Federal Britain

This publication is based on research that forms part of the Paragon Initiative.

This five-year project will provide a fundamental reassessment of what government should – and should not – do. It will put every area of government activity under the microscope and analyse the failure of current policies.

The project will put forward clear and considered solutions to the UK's problems. It will also identify the areas of government activity that can be put back into the hands of individuals, families, civil society, local government, charities and markets.

The Paragon Initiative will create a blueprint for a better, freer Britain – and provide a clear vision of a new relationship between the state and society.

FEDERAL BRITAIN

The Case for Decentralisation

PHILIP BOOTH

Institute of
Economic Affairs

First published in Great Britain in 2015 by
The Institute of Economic Affairs
2 Lord North Street
Westminster
London SW1P 3LB
in association with London Publishing Partnership Ltd
www.londonpublishingpartnership.co.uk

Many IEA publications are translated into languages other than English or are reprinted. Permission to translate or to reprint should be sought from the Director General at the address above.

Typeset in Kepler by T&T Productions Ltd
www.tandtproductions.com

Printed and bound in Great Britain by Page Bros

CONTENTS

THE AUTHOR

Philip Booth

Philip Booth is Editorial and Programme Director at the Institute of Economic Affairs and Professor of Finance, Public Policy and Ethics at St Mary's University, Twickenham. Previously, he was Professor of Insurance and Risk Management at Cass Business School. He also worked for the Bank of England as an advisor on financial stability issues and has been Associate Dean of Cass Business School. He has written widely, including a number of books, on investment, finance, social insurance and pensions as well as on the relationship between Catholic social teaching and economics. Philip has a BA in economics from the University of Durham and a PhD from City University. He is a Fellow of the Institute of Actuaries and a Fellow of the Royal Statistical Society.

FOREWORD

Relative to many other states, the United Kingdom over the last century has been a highly successful multinational polity. Even the tragic Troubles of Northern Ireland paled in comparison with the ethnic and religious conflicts that have torn apart so many other nations. Historically, the British have often been sceptical of American and continental European proclivities for trying to solve political problems with formal constitutional arrangements. They have instead usually preferred the more informal British tradition of muddling through under the nation's unwritten constitution. Most of the time that tradition has arguably served the UK well.

In recent years, however, the future viability of the UK has been called into question by the growing conflict between relatively left-wing Scots and the more right-of-centre electorate in England. Although independence was defeated in the September 2014 Scottish referendum, secessionist sentiment might well be rekindled in the aftermath of the Conservative Party's surprising victory in the 2015 UK election, which also saw massive gains for the pro-independence Scottish National Party in Scotland. As English and Scottish views on the role of government in society become increasingly divergent, the pressure on the UK political system might well increase, perhaps even to breaking point.

These developments have led many to consider the possibility that Britain might need some more formal system of federalism to survive. Proposals for a more federal and decentralised UK have been advanced on both the left and the right in the hope that they might resolve the seeming impasse in which the nation finds itself. The ultimate resolution of these issues is important not only to the peoples of Britain, but also to many elsewhere. A successful settlement of the UK's constitutional issues might well be a model from which others can learn. It might also create important benefits for Britain's partners in the European Union, and its overseas allies, including my own country. Failure might have ripple effects on the European Union and beyond.

Philip Booth's important contribution to the debate over Britain's constitutional future is both timely and insightful. As he effectively demonstrates, a greater decentralisation of power in Britain might not only reduce the intensity of political conflict, but also strengthen the economy, and offer English, Scots, Welsh and Northern Irish alike a greater range of political choice through foot voting. Britons of all national groups would have enhanced opportunities to live under the policies they prefer by voting with their feet for those jurisdictions that adopt them. As he outlines, foot voters generally have better incentives to make informed and logical decisions than conventional ballot box voters.

Booth also effectively argues that devolution of power works best if coupled with a matching devolution of fiscal responsibility. Local and regional authorities will not have good incentives to adopt effective policies unless they must pay for them out of their own tax revenue. If a local or regional government can force taxpayers elsewhere to pay for its mistakes, it is likely to make more of them. It will also have much weaker incentives to adopt policies that are attractive to taxpaying citizens. By contrast, a government that must raise its own revenue sources has a strong incentive to compete for residents by adopting policies that are both cost-conscious and effective.

The result of such competition and foot voting will not automatically be a small-government, libertarian-oriented polity. Interventionist regions might also prosper in inter-jurisdictional competition if their higher levels of taxation and regulation create sufficient off-setting benefits to attract residents and investors. The key point is that both left- and right-wing sub-national governments will have to find ways to make themselves more attractive to foot voters.

Few will agree with every single detail of Booth's proposal. Ultimately, any successful federal system for Britain will have to be the product of negotiation between the different regions and peoples of the UK. Not even the best and most insightful academics and policy analysts can fully predict the details of such a settlement in advance.

But Philip Booth's paper is an outstanding contribution to the discussion of these issues, and deserves careful consideration from those interested in the constitutional future of Britain.

ILYA SOMIN
Law professor at George Mason University and author of
Democracy and Political Ignorance: Why Smaller Government Is Smarter

October 2015

The views expressed in this monograph are, as in all IEA publications, those of the author and not those of the Institute (which has no corporate view), its managing trustees, Academic Advisory Council members or senior staff. With some exceptions, such as with the publication of lectures, all IEA monographs are blind peer-reviewed by at least two academics or researchers who are experts in the field. Because this publication was written by the Editorial Director, the Chairman of the Academic Advisory Council, Professor Martin Ricketts, was also involved in the review process.

ACKNOWLEDGEMENT

I thank Tom Packer and Matt Sinclair for the ideas they contributed to the decentralisation of local government sections, and Diego Zuluaga Laguna, who wrote much of the chapter on international examples. I also thank various reviewers who provided helpful comments.

SUMMARY

- The United Kingdom's current devolution settlement
  leads to unrepresentative government and has an
  inbuilt bias towards 'big government'. This situation
  is exacerbated because nations with devolved
  government are over-represented in the UK parliament
  compared with their population, when it might be
  expected that they would be under-represented.
- The UK has the most centralised government of the
  G7, as measured by the proportion of revenue raised
  by sub-central government. In the UK, only 5 per cent
  of revenue is raised locally, compared with 50 per cent
  in Canada and 13 per cent in France, which is the next
  most centralised country by this measure.
- Measured by the proportion of total government
  spending undertaken by sub-central government, the
  UK does not fare quite as badly. However, it is among
  a group of three countries in which between 20 and
  30 per cent of all government spending takes place
  at sub-central central government levels – this is
  much less than the G7 average. A further indication
  of the degree of centralisation in the UK is the fact
  that, in 2011, local authorities had over 1,300 statutory
  duties laid down by parliament. In other words, local
  government has substantial spending responsibilities,

but very often these involve fulfilling statutory obligations.

- There are a number of benefits from decentralising government, e.g. it promotes greater experimentation, better matching of services to local preferences and greater competition between providers of government-funded services.

- Theory is confirmed by the evidence. Fiscal decentralisation is associated with higher national income, better school performance and higher levels of investment. In particular, the decentralisation of revenue-raising powers has a stronger effect on performance than the decentralisation of spending. The evidence suggests that increasing the local share of taxation from 5 per cent to 20 per cent (still low by G7 standards) could raise GDP per capita by 6 per cent. With especially low levels of revenue decentralisation, and as a large country, the UK is in a particularly good position to gain from transferring powers and revenue-raising responsibilities from central to local government.

- The UK needs to reform in two areas. Firstly, a federal state should be created with Scotland and either the rest of the UK (RUK), or England, Wales and Northern Ireland separately, becoming nations within a federal union. The federal government should have a very limited number of powers including defence, foreign affairs and border control and a small parliament and executive. No other proposed solution to the 'English question' can provide the same stability or beneficial economic outcomes. Secondly, there should be radical decentralisation of powers within Scotland and RUK to local government. The principle that should be followed is that of 'subsidiarity': this does not mean central government pushing powers downwards while keeping ultimate control. Rather, control should be at the local level unless functions cannot be performed locally. Current UK government proposals to devolve powers to cities do not deal with the problems identified by this research and may well exacerbate them.

- Federal states have a tendency towards centralisation, the US being an important example. Centralisation would be prevented by requiring unanimity among the parliaments of all the individual nations as well as agreement of the federal parliament before any further powers were passed to the federal (UK) level.

- Within the federal nations, responsibility for the following should be transferred from national government to the local level: environmental policy; working-age welfare; education and health; granting of permissions for and regulation of natural resource exploitation; lifestyle regulation; policing; and housing and planning. Local authorities could join together to provide some functions, such as policing, where local geography or other circumstances make that desirable. In addition, there should be complementary reforms to promote autonomy for individuals, families and civil society institutions, especially in relation to health and education.

- Except for working-age welfare, which would be largely financed by government grant but administered by local government, all local government functions would be financed entirely by local revenue streams. These would come from user charges and from some combination of the following, to be determined at local level: taxes modelled on the current council tax; land value taxes; taxes on business property; natural resource levies; consumption taxes; variation in income taxes; and tourist taxes.

- Two crucial principles must be applied when implementing these proposals. Firstly, revenue must be raised by the layer of government that is undertaking spending. Secondly, one layer of government must not bail out the debts incurred by any other layer of government. To prevent the problems seen in the euro zone, the central bank would not accept Scottish or RUK (or English, Welsh and Northern Irish if appropriate) bonds as collateral in monetary policy operations.

TABLES, FIGURES AND BOXES

1   INTRODUCTION

The current UK constitutional arrangements with regard to devolution and local government are a mess. In itself, this might not be a problem. Many aspects of the UK government have evolved rather than being rationally designed. That is the nature of a country without a written constitution and which has a common law tradition. However, in the case of devolution and local government, there has not been a process of evolution designed to deal with problems as they arise, but rather a gradual centralisation (in the case of local government functions) together with asymmetric reform (in the case of devolution) that has resulted from political pressures and actions borne more from opportunism than from principle or an analysis of the economic costs and benefits.

No comparable country is as centralised as the UK when it comes to the distribution of functions and revenue-raising powers between central and local government. We also have a devolution settlement which gives wide-ranging powers to some parts of the UK and not others, and which separates decisions about spending from the consequences of those decisions in terms of the necessary levels of taxation.

Problems with the UK constitutional settlement

Devolution

The UK's devolution settlement has created a situation in which large numbers of members of parliament vote on matters that do not concern their constituents. In other words, there is representation without taxation, rather like in the case of rotten and pocket boroughs before the 1832 Reform Act. It also happens that those nations of Britain that tend to be more supportive of higher levels of regulation and government spending have the greatest number of devolved powers. This creates an asymmetric bias in the UK parliament towards higher levels of government intervention. If the UK as a whole votes for a low-spending government, Scotland, Wales and Northern Ireland can still choose a high-spending government. On the other hand, if England votes for a low-spending government (as indicated by a majority of MPs being elected in England for a party that wishes to reduce government spending), it may well have a high-spending government imposed on it by electors in Scotland, Wales and Northern Ireland.

By any metric, the nations to which powers have been devolved have much higher levels of government spending than England. The non-English MPs have an incentive to try to maintain such levels of spending and to increase spending further if that spending will not be financed by their constituents. Of course, any MP has an incentive to try to ensure more spending on things that benefit their constituents that is financed by taxpayers in general (see, for example, Tullock

1976). However, the interests of the non-English MPs are strongly aligned around this particular objective. They all have a very strong interest in maintaining the current government spending settlement whereby additional spending outside England is financed by taxpayers in general (that is, mainly by English taxpayers). When such a large body of representatives has strongly aligned interests around a single objective, it is much more difficult to prevent it achieving its goals – this is particularly so if that group holds the balance of power in parliament. Indeed, throughout the last 30 years, we have seen a number of particular concessions to the Celtic nations of the UK, including promises that have been made by the current government not to reform the Barnett formula, which determines government spending in the UK nations.

These problems are further exacerbated by the fact that Scotland, Wales and Northern Ireland are over-represented in the UK parliament despite many of the decisions made by that parliament having no bearing on those nations. For example, in England, there are nearly 30 per cent more electors per parliamentary seat than there are in Wales. Thus, an extra impetus is given to the big government bias.

Overall, therefore, the devolution settlement creates unrepresentative government and is likely to create a bias towards big government.

Local government and fiscal centralisation

As measured by the proportion of revenue raised by sub-central government, the UK has the most centralised political system of all comparable countries. In the UK, just 5 per cent of revenue is raised by local government. The figures in other countries range from 13 per cent in France to 50 per cent in Canada.

Such a level of fiscal centralisation gives rise to a number of difficulties. The first is that the package of goods and services – in terms of both the amount of goods and services provided and the make-up of that package – cannot be easily varied according to local need. For example, it is highly likely that the form of assistance that should be given to unemployed people in Huntingdon would be very different from the form of assistance that needs to be given to the unemployed in Hackney in London. Preferences when it comes to education, the regulation of activities such as shopping, gambling or drinking, and so on, will also vary across the country.

Moreover, because the system is so centralised, local government cannot be disciplined by constituents moving between local government areas. It is much easier for people to move from, for example, Oxford to Banbury or from Bristol to Taunton than it is to leave the country altogether. The absence of what is described below as foot voting leads to three further problems. Firstly, an important discipline on government is lost, both in terms of providing higher-quality services and also in terms of providing services at the lowest possible cost in terms of taxation. Secondly, knowledge about the preferences of voters is less easily communicated to their representatives. Thirdly, there is likely to be a lack of experimentation and the copying and diffusion of good practice. Indeed, any differences between local provision in different areas is often heavily criticised by the media and such differences were named 'postcode lotteries' by the Blair governments. The other side of allowing differences, however, is that services can be better matched to local preferences and there is an incentive for services to be better everywhere even if there are differences in performance.

These theoretical problems with centralisation are confirmed by the evidence. In the limited situations where foot voting can be exercised, residents are indeed active. It is clear that local residents do move house – and pay a premium – in order to live in the catchment areas of better schools. The detailed empirical studies suggest that fiscal decentralisation leads to better economic outcomes as measured by factor productivity, investment, school performance and national income. Of course, many of the benefits of decentralisation, such as better public services or public services being better matched to the preferences of residents, will not be captured by statistical studies because national income statistics tend to measure the contribution of public services to national income by counting inputs rather than by assessing the value of outputs to residents.

One study discussed below, for example, finds that doubling the share of sub-central taxes or spending shares is likely to be associated with an increase in per capita GDP of around 3 per cent. The same author suggests that, if the UK raised the same proportion of tax revenue at the sub-national level as Sweden, it would increase national income by 4 per cent. The evidence can best be summed up by the Lyons report into local government financing, which concluded (Lyons 2007: Executive Summary 33):

> Recent work comparing the UK with the USA and Europe has concluded that the lack of devolution and local discretion in the UK is a constraint on economic performance, particularly in the cities.

Interestingly, the academic evidence suggests that the UK has the worst of all possible circumstances – revenue raising is much more centralised than spending. The evidence suggests that this combination tends to lead to higher levels of government spending. This is not surprising given the lack of accountability that would exist within such a system. Furthermore, if local government is simply spending central government grants, it becomes a powerful lobby group lobbying for higher grants, rather than a part of government raising revenue to provide services valued by its citizens.

Both theory and evidence suggest that, with its high levels of revenue centralisation combined with moderate levels of spending centralisation, the UK is in an especially good position to benefit from reform. What should be done?

UK constitutional reform and decentralisation

Constitutional reform

This paper proposes a federal solution to the UK devolution dilemma. Scotland and the rest of the UK (RUK) would form two nations within a federal structure; alternatively,

Scotland and any combination of England, Wales and Northern Ireland either together or separately could be the nations within a federal structure. Which nations would be independent within the federal structure would be decided at the outset by the electorates of Scotland, Wales and Northern Ireland. For ease of exposition, it will be assumed that the nations within the federal structure are Scotland and RUK.

The federal government would have responsibility for a very small number of functions, such as defence, foreign affairs and the management of the existing debt. These would be financed by a specific federal tax. There would be a small federal executive and a small federal parliament that would meet not nearly as frequently as the current UK parliament. To prevent centralisation, which has been a huge difficulty in federal arrangements, such as the US, and in intergovernmental arrangements, such as the EU, unanimous agreement of all the nations within the federal structure as well as agreement of the federal parliament would be necessary for further powers to be passed up to the federal level. It would be the lower levels of government that would decide what was passed up to the higher levels, not the other way round.

This arrangement would remove all the anomalies and asymmetries within the current devolution settlement. It would also ensure that each level of government and each nation was entirely responsible for raising revenue for all the functions for which they were responsible. There would be strict rules in relation to borrowing at both the national and federal levels.

Decentralisation

The federal system would mean that the individual nations (Scotland and RUK) were responsible for other government functions such as health, education, welfare and most forms of regulation. This would encompass the lion's share of government spending. It is then further proposed that there is radical decentralisation within the nations that constitute the federal UK. Specifically, the following functions would become the responsibility of local levels of government in addition to their current functions:

- environmental policy
- working-age welfare
- education and health
- natural resource exploitation
- lifestyle regulation
- policing
- housing and planning

This list is not exhaustive. For example, some aspects of road transport that are not currently a local responsibility could become so. Also, one of these areas is currently already a local responsibility but is administered in such a way that proper accountability is impossible (policing). In the case of some of these policy areas, there would be complementary policies that involved even greater decentralisation. For example, with regard to education, parents would be financed directly and the local government role would be a residual one. Except for working-age welfare, which would be financed by government grant but administered by local government, all of these functions, together with existing local government functions, would be financed entirely by local revenue streams from some combination of the following taxes determined at local level:

- taxes modelled on the current council tax
- land value taxes
- taxes on business property
- natural resource levies
- consumption taxes
- tourist taxes
- (possibly) income taxes set at the local level but collected nationally

The relationship between revenue raising and spending would then be very clear.

Decentralisation would be combined with strict rules to ensure that local government debt was controlled and that local government was explicitly accountable for its own debt. Further decentralisation to lower levels of local government would be encouraged.

Overall, this is a radical programme of reform that both theory and evidence suggest is capable of transforming the political economy of Britain as well as producing much better economic outcomes. Other proposals, such as 'English votes for English laws' in the UK parliament or reducing the number of Scottish MPs either do not properly address the current problems or would have side effects that would make the overall constitutional settlement worse.

Furthermore, despite the ad hoc proposals for decentralisation to some areas, such as Manchester, there have been no serious proposals for comprehensive decentralisation or for revenue-raising decentralisation by the current government.[1] A reversal of the process of centralisation that has been going on for at least 80 years in the UK is urgently needed.

The principle that would be embedded in these reforms is that of subsidiarity. This is a concept much misused and misunderstood, especially in the EU. It has its roots in Catholic social teaching and can be described as follows:[2]

> it is an injustice and at the same time a grave evil and disturbance of right order to assign to a greater and higher association what lesser and subordinate organizations can do.

Note that the principle argues that smaller organisations should be allowed to do what they can do, not what they are most efficient at doing – this implies, among other things, that the benefit of the doubt should be in the direction of decentralisation. This suggests that the decentralisation to local government proposed here should not necessarily be the end of the process.

The approach to federalism described here has the potential to embrace the principle of subsidiarity fully.

---

1 Even the much heralded decentralisation of business rates announced in October 2015 comes with many caveats.

2 *Quadragesimo anno*, 79. See http://w2.vatican.va/content/pius-xi/en/encyclicals/documents/hf_p-xi_enc_19310515_quadragesimo-anno.html

Powers could only be moved upwards if the nations within the federal UK decided by unanimity that they could not perform the relevant function themselves. The EU would have much to gain from applying the principle of subsidiarity properly. The UK – which currently is hardly in a position to complain about centralisation within the EU – should lead the way.

2 LOCAL GOVERNMENT AND DEVOLUTION: THE BRITISH CONSTITUTIONAL SETTLEMENT

Devolution – the background

The UK has been characterised by various forms of devolution throughout its history. However, there was a step change in 1999, when the Scottish Parliament and Welsh Assembly were formed. Just before that, in 1998, devolved government returned to Northern Ireland. The powers that have been devolved to each of the nations are not the same, and the different nations have used them in different ways.

In Scotland, the following matters are devolved:[1]

- health and social work
- education and training
- local government and housing
- justice and policing
- agriculture, forestry and fisheries
- the environment
- tourism, sport and heritage
- economic development and internal transport

---

1 https://www.gov.uk/devolution-settlement-scotland

Spending decisions, organisational issues and the passing of primary legislation in these areas have all been devolved. The devolved matters cover a large proportion of government activity, with the major exception of welfare. By comparison with spending powers, however, revenue-raising powers are limited. The original devolution settlement, and then the Scotland Act 2012, gave the Scottish government the power to vary income tax and also vary some other, minor taxes. However, revenue raising is essentially still a matter for the UK government.

Following the referendum on Scottish independence in September 2014, further proposals were made for devolution. The measures that were proposed by the Conservative Party in the 2015 election campaign included requiring that 50 per cent of revenue spent in Scotland was raised in Scotland and also the devolution of welfare and further health and social matters. These proposals were adopted in the Scotland Bill. At time of writing, this is going through parliament and will give the Scottish parliament control over income tax rates and bands, a half share in Scottish value added tax (VAT) revenues and a greater say over welfare policy in Scotland. These measures could reduce the extent of fiscal centralisation within the UK, but they are also likely to exacerbate the problems caused by asymmetries in the devolution settlement, which are discussed below. It was also proposed in the Conservative manifesto that the Barnett formula (see below) should be maintained and that a special funding floor for Wales should be introduced.

As far as spending and the delivery of services are concerned, the devolved powers to Wales and Northern

Ireland are not significantly different from those in Scotland. However, the powers to enact legislation are less wide-ranging and there is no control of income tax.

The devolution settlements mirror the arrangements within local government in England in that there is far more devolution of spending than of revenue raising. As will be discussed below, this is probably the worst of all possible combinations.

Local government and fiscal centralisation in the UK – the background

The UK has something of a 'patchwork' system of local government. That is not necessarily a bad thing. Different approaches to local government may well be appropriate in different areas – for example, in urban as compared with rural areas. This paper does not propose a reorganisation of the structures of local government. Rather, the focus of discussion is on the extent to which local government should have greater responsibilities devolved from the centre.

In England, there are 55 single-tier authorities that have responsibility for nearly all local government matters. In addition there are 27 non-metropolitan counties, which tend to be large areas that have responsibility for education, libraries and a number of other areas of expenditure over which it is believed that more strategic oversight is needed. These counties also contain lower-tier authorities responsible for services such as refuse collection and planning applications. There are additional complexities within this system. For example, there are a number of metropolitan boroughs which tend to act as unitary authorities. Also, the local government arrangements in London are quite different from those that exist in the rest of the country. There are a few functions undertaken by parish or town councils, which tend to represent very small areas and have advisory functions as well as some spending powers.

There are ongoing attempts to decentralise authority in a piecemeal way. For example, there are ad hoc arrangements such as City Deals. These do not address the problems discussed below and, indeed, do not in any meaningful way lead to decentralisation. Those areas involved in City Deals often have greater freedom as to how they spend government grants. However, they are also able to borrow for the purposes of spending more on areas where less spending would previously have taken place – thus taking economic power from the private sector and increasing the power of local government relative to the private sector. Furthermore, many of the powers that are being given to local authority areas under City Deals involve increased regulation of areas of economic life that had been deregulated under previous governments. City Deals also often involve moving powers from lower levels of local government to more distant levels: for example, in the Leeds City Deal, five local authorities are going to move to a combined authority model.[2] There is no genuine attempt under this programme to decentralise revenue

---

2   See the government document detailing all the City Deals: https://www.gov.uk/government/uploads/system/uploads/attachment_data/file/221009/Guide-to-City-Deals-wave-1.pdf

raising and spending from central to local government. In general, City Deals lead to higher levels of spending and regulation of local economic activity than would otherwise have taken place.

Local authority spending under central government control

Councils have wide-ranging but constrained powers. For example, they are responsible for: children's services (though not free schools and academies); aspects of highways and transport; social care for adults; housing; planning; the environment; and fire and rescue services.[3] They also have some role in the provision of other services that are coordinated locally but for which they are not directly responsible, such as policing.

In many of these areas, local discretion is limited and most local authorities are implementing national government guidelines or plans. An indication of local government's subservient role is given by the fact that, in 2011, there were over 1,300 local authority statutory duties.[4]

Thus, the provision of services is heavily circumscribed and regulated. By way of example, local authority schools must follow the national curriculum, and libraries are subject to the 1964 Public Libraries and Museums Act (Chapter 75), in which it states:

3   http://www.local.gov.uk/c/document_library/get_file?uuid=a5b2c920
    -8f40-4eae-9852-8b983724f5bc&groupId=10180

4   https://www.gov.uk/government/publications/review-of-local
    -government-statutory-duties-summary-of-responses--2

it shall be the duty of the Secretary of State to superintend, and promote the improvement of, the public library service provided by local authorities in England and Wales, and to secure the proper discharge by local authorities of the functions in relation to libraries conferred on them as library authorities by or under this Act.

As far as the provision of adult and children's services is concerned, local authorities effectively carry out legislative duties as laid down in acts of parliament. There is even a special government fund to enable local authorities to empty dustbins once a week rather than once a fortnight.

The centralisation of revenue raising

When it comes to taxation, or revenue raising, the extent of central control is even greater than that over spending. Furthermore, the modest decentralisation to areas such as Manchester barely affects revenue raising.

Even the one tax that is levied and determined by local councils is heavily regulated by central government. The government provided funding of £5.2 billion between 2010 and 2015 to freeze council tax,[5] and councils are unable to update valuations, use alternative taxes or even change the council tax banding system within a local area. There is even less local discretion with regard to business rates,

---

5   https://www.gov.uk/government/publications/2010-to-2015-government -policy-council-tax-reform/2010-to-2015-government-policy-council-tax -reform

the other main tax designed to finance local government, which is administered and set by central government, though business rates will be deregulated somewhat under proposals made in October 2015.

Measured by the percentage of tax revenue raised at sub-national level, the UK has by far the lowest level of tax autonomy for local government among comparable countries. According to Organisation for Economic Co-operation and Development (OECD) figures, in 2011, 4.8 per cent of all tax was raised locally. This is on a par with (or slightly higher than) Slovakia and the Netherlands, which are much smaller than the UK. Countries that are more similar to the UK raise much more of their taxes below central government level as a proportion of the total tax take. For example, France (13 per cent), Italy (16 per cent), the US (37 per cent) and Germany (29 per cent) all raise a significantly greater proportion of total taxes at sub-national level than the UK (see Table 1).

As can be seen in Table 1, which includes all G7 countries, the figures for expenditure (except Japan, for which such figures are not available) tell a different story. When it comes to the extent of government spending administered below central government level, the UK is at the low end of the spectrum, but not an outlier; though, as noted, local government spending is heavily regulated. It is also interesting to note that, as far as we can tell from available figures, there is a remarkable consistency in the percentage of spending at the local level in Italy and France at the two dates 1890 and 2013. On the other hand, there has been a dramatic fall in the UK.

Table 1   Percentage of tax revenue and government spending at sub-national level

Country	Percentage of tax revenue raised at sub-national level 2013	Percentage of expenditure at sub-national level 2013	Percentage of expenditure at sub-national level 1890
UK	5	25	43
France	13	21	22
Italy	16	28	25
Japan	25	—	—
Germany	29	39	—
US	37	48	62
Canada	50	67	—

Figures for 2013 from OECD Fiscal Decentralisation Database; figures for 1890 from Bastable (1895) – there are some potential inaccuracies in the figure for France and there may be different definitions used.

Problems caused by the devolution settlement

There are a number of problems with the UK's devolution settlement.

Big government asymmetrical bias

The current political settlement in the UK is asymmetrical in the sense that some MPs have responsibility for determining legislation that does not affect their constituents: in other words, we have representation without taxation. This, in itself, is not necessarily a problem as long as there are accountability and proper checks and balances within the system to prevent such biases significantly affecting

19

government decisions. However, in the case of the UK, a form of devolution has evolved that has a built-in bias towards higher levels of government spending than the electorate may desire.

The political bias within the UK system is perhaps best explained with reference to what became known as the West Lothian question. This was raised by Tam Dalyell, Member of Parliament for West Lothian, when debating the Labour government devolution proposals in 1977. The problem manifests itself or can be expressed in various ways. For example, Scottish members of parliament can vote on matters that only pertain to England and that have no effect on their own constituents. Such MPs are rather like MPs from rotten or pocket boroughs before the 1832 Reform Act – the members are not accountable to anybody for the decisions they take on a wide range of devolved issues, but they can affect policy in constituencies that do not elect them.

It is difficult to predict the impact of this situation on MPs' voting behaviour. If MPs do not have vested interests to protect because a given decision does not affect their constituents, they might be less likely to vote for interventionist measures. However, the nations to which there has been devolution tend to have high levels of government spending relative to taxation. Their MPs would have an incentive to maintain high levels of spending not financed by their own constituents. Furthermore, under the party whipping system, Scottish MPs can simply be required to vote with their English colleagues, though this is less of a problem since May 2015 as there are only three Scottish MPs who are not members of the Scottish National Party. MPs in devolved nations tend disproportionately to be members of parties that believe in greater levels of government spending. As such, these MPs can vote for more government spending in England (which they do not represent and which may not want more government spending) while also being confident that there will be a majority favourable to high levels of government spending in the assemblies or parliaments of their own nations.

As Packer and Sinclair (2015) pointed out, electorates in devolved areas tend to be more likely to favour greater government intervention. This also creates an asymmetric bias in the UK parliament towards higher levels of government spending. If the UK as a whole votes for a low-spending government, Scotland, Wales and Northern Ireland – and perhaps representatives in those parts of England that have some devolved powers – can still choose a high-spending government. On the other hand, if England votes for a low-spending government (as indicated by a majority of MPs being elected in England for a party that wishes to reduce government spending), it may well have a high-spending government imposed on it by electors in the nations to which powers have been devolved.

This problem is illustrated by the results of a YouGov survey in which participants were asked for their view on whether the level of spending and taxes should be higher, lower or around the same. Voters in Scotland were more likely than those in the UK as a whole to say they would

Figure 1 The money the government spends on public services and other things comes mainly from taxation. Do you think...

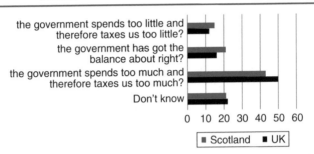

Total sample size was 1,684 adults. Fieldwork was undertaken 10–11 March 2013 by YouGov for the TaxPayers' Alliance. The survey was carried out online. The figures were weighted and are representative of all GB adults (aged 18+). Taken directly from Packer and Sinclair (2015).

prefer higher spending and taxes, and less likely to prefer lower spending and taxes (see Figure 1).

Over-representation of Scotland, Wales and Northern Ireland

The problem of asymmetry is compounded by over-representation in the UK parliament of those nations with devolved powers. It might be expected that nations with devolved powers would have fewer members of the UK parliament, but the opposite is the case. Using 2013 figures, the mean and median number of electors per seat is shown in Table 2.

All the other home nations have higher representation than England. In turn, Wales and Northern Ireland have

Table 2   Electors per seat in the UK nations

Nation	Total number of electors	Total number of seats	Mean electors per seat	Median electors per seat
England	38,587,100	533	72,396	72,400
Scotland	4,027,200	59	68,258	69,000
Wales	2,297,300	40	57,433	56,800
Northern Ireland	1,218,400	18	67,689	66,800

greater representation than Scotland because their devolution settlements involved the transfer of fewer powers.

Historically, there has been some attempt to alter the number of seats allocated between the four nations to take account of the extent of devolution. For example, Northern Ireland had 13 (reduced to 12) seats during the period of devolved power up to 1974. This was then increased after direct rule was imposed. The number of Scottish seats was also reduced, from 72 to 59, before the 2005 general election to reflect its increased devolved powers. Nevertheless, Scotland is still over-represented.

Even if the representation of Scotland, Wales and Northern Ireland is not decisive in determining the government of the UK as a whole, it can still affect the balance of opinion in parliament. There have been times, however, when the election results in the nations that now have devolved powers were decisive. Though Scotland did not have devolved powers at that time, in October 1974 the Labour Party's majority in Scotland was far bigger than its majority in the UK as a whole. In 2010, the Conservative Party had a very clear overall majority in England but not in the UK.

High government spending in Scotland, Wales and Northern Ireland

It has been argued above that the devolution settlement is asymmetrical and favours those parts of the UK that have supported a larger state. This, in turn, means that there will be an artificial bias that will encourage high spending and high levels of regulation. High spending in the nations that have devolution pre-dated the current settlement and it is difficult to argue that devolution is the cause of high spending in Scotland, Wales and Northern Ireland. However, the devolution settlement makes it more likely that this situation will continue into the future.

The level of government spending in 2004–5 in the UK, England, Scotland, Wales and Northern Ireland is given in Table 3 as a proportion of national income at factor cost (the most appropriate measure of national income for such comparisons). Other figures are given for employment in the public sector and also more recent figures for government spending per head (in absolute terms and as a percentage of the UK average).

Government spending is clearly much higher in the nations with devolved government. One possible explanation is that, from long before devolution, Scottish, Welsh and Northern Irish representatives in parliament comprised well-aligned interest groups[6] that could obtain benefits while spreading the costs over the whole electorate[7].

---

6   Applying the argument of Olson (1965).

7   Very particular examples of this include, in 1979, discussions (which broke down) between Ulster Unionists and the UK government over the provision of cheap energy in exchange for support in a confidence motion, and

Table 3   Government spending in the UK nations

	Government spending as % of GDP 2004–5	Proportion of workforce in the public sector 2004–5	Government spending on services per head (£) 2012–13	Government spending on services per head as % of UK average 2012–13
England	46.0	19.5	8,529	97.1
Scotland	58.5	23.8	10,152	115.5
Wales	67.9	23.3	9,709	110.5
Northern Ireland	75.8	29.8	10,876	123.8
UK	47.2	20.3	8,788	100

Source: Smith (2006) and Public Expenditure Statistical Analyses (2014, Chapter 9).

Having gained such concessions, the devolution settlement gives an incentive to the electorate and their representatives to maintain and enhance them.

This problem is exacerbated because, when it comes to the UK parliament, non-English MPs have interests in a relatively small number of issues – the general fiscal settlement being one of them. This is because most issues of importance have been devolved, while the raising of finances to fund the devolved spending has not been devolved. The interests of the non-English MPs are likely to be closely aligned around the objective of maintaining or improving their fiscal settlement. Even members of the UK

concessions to Plaid Cymru which, did, in fact, secure their support in that no confidence vote. See http://www.walesonline.co.uk/news/wales-news/could-worse-gordon-think-callaghan-2120651. In the 1979 general election, both major parties promised a dedicated Welsh language television channel and the leader of Plaid Cymru threatened to go on hunger strike if the promise was not delivered.

parliament who believed in cutting government spending in general may support increases in government spending for their nations, given that the cost would be spread across the UK.

This combination of policies – pre-existing high levels of government spending outside England, very little responsibility for raising the taxes necessary to fund the spending and the closely aligned interests of non-English members of the UK parliament around the maintenance of high spending outside England – compounds the problems of political asymmetry in the devolution settlement. All of these problems point in the direction of encouraging the growth of the size of government.

3   THE PROBLEMS OF FISCAL CENTRALISATION AND THE BENEFITS OF DECENTRALISATION

Tiebout sorting

One of the main economic roles of government is the responsibility for the provision of public goods that cannot easily be provided privately.[1] The Tiebout (1956) model, often known as Tiebout sorting, suggests that there can be considerable advantages of fiscal decentralisation. Decentralisation allows local government units to offer different packages of public goods that are suited to the different preferences of local residents. Thus, decentralisation allows for differences between preferences – the residents of Buckingham do not necessarily want the same set of public goods as the residents of Liverpool.

Localisation also ensures that local knowledge can be exploited by politicians and bureaucrats when determining the desired form of government provision. Furthermore, local governments can be disciplined by residents, who can move between local areas, thus putting pressure on localities to provide the right level and

---

1   Of course, there is substantial evidence that many goods and services that are often called 'public' goods are often 'club' goods and can be provided privately. However, we do not pursue that debate here.

combination of public goods (see 'foot voting' below). As Tiebout puts it: 'Spatial mobility provides the local public-goods counterpart to the private market's shopping trip' (Tiebout 1956: 422) and 'While the solution may not be perfect because of institutional rigidities, this does not invalidate its importance' (ibid.: 424). In addition, tax competition can complement competition in public good provision and both can help keep government more efficient and ensure more appropriate provision of public goods. This can work both at the UK level (competition between Scotland and RUK or the other constituent nations) and at the more local level.

Confused representation and voter ignorance

The problem of rational ignorance among electorates is widely discussed. In general, voters do not have a strong incentive to acquire economic and political knowledge because there is an infinitesimal probability that their votes will affect an election. However, interest groups that are well organised and that might have an opportunity to change policy have an incentive to campaign and become well informed (again, see Olson 1965). This view is challenged by, for example, Byran Caplan (2007), who argues that, rather than suffering from rational ignorance, voters are irrational and possess several inherent biases that would tend to lead to bad policy (for example, biases towards protectionism).

It would appear to be true that there are straightforward objective issues that voters get wrong or do not understand. These are not just issues in relation to economic policy. Voters do not even understand for which areas of policy the politicians for whom they are voting are responsible. Somin (2013) cites some examples relating to the US:

- In 2006, only 42 per cent of Americans could name the three branches of government.
- In the 2010 election, nearly two-thirds of the US electorate got the wrong answer when asked if the economy had grown in that year.
- In the 2010 election, less than half the electorate knew that the Republicans controlled the House of Representatives but not the senate.

In the UK, there are similar findings. For example, an Ipsos–MORI poll uncovered the following:[2]

- Nearly 30 per cent of people think the government spends more on jobseekers' allowance than on pensions, when in fact the government spends fifteen times more on pensions.
- Over one-quarter of people think that foreign aid is one of the top two or three items of government spending when it actually made up just over 1 per cent of government spending in the 2011/12 financial year.

These issues form the battleground for many political debates in the UK around election time.

---

2   https://www.ipsos-mori.com/researchpublications/researcharchive/
    3188/Perceptions-are-not-reality-the-top-10-we-get-wrong.aspx

In many senses, it does not matter whether voters are rationally ignorant while interest groups are rationally well informed and therefore unduly influence policy or whether voters are simply irrational; the policy conclusion is the same: we should rely as little as possible on the political system for delivering economic goals.

Unfortunately, the UK political system is especially well designed to exacerbate the effects of voter ignorance.

Firstly, our system is complex. It is possible, in England, to vote in the elections for the following layers of government, all of which exercise some power: European Union; UK parliament; county council; district council; parish or town council. In some parts of the country, some of these layers do not exist or are replaced with different layers, but in many parts of the country there are five layers of government – four of which only raise 5 per cent of revenue between them. In Scotland, Wales and Northern Ireland there are also devolved authorities, though the structure of local government is somewhat different. This complexity compounds the voter ignorance problem: it is simply more difficult for voters to understand who controls what. Avoiding complexity does not mean that different approaches to local government should not be used in different areas of the country. Complexity of the system as a whole matters less than complexity of the arrangements relating to a particular local government area.

The system of government in the UK is also highly centralised, as discussed above. This leads to two further problems related to voter ignorance. The larger the governmental unit, the smaller the chance of an individual elector influencing an election, so individuals have less incentive to be well informed. In addition to this, as has been noted, the UK is much more highly centralised when it comes to revenue raising than with regard to spending. Moreover, spending is often localised in theory, but in practice it is dictated by government guidelines and regulation. All of these factors make it much more difficult to ascertain which layer of government is responsible for what functions.

The following approaches could ameliorate the problem of voter ignorance:

- Limiting the functions of government so that individuals and civil society organisations are responsible for a greater number of important economic decisions. This makes it easier to assess the performance of government over the narrower range of activities for which it is responsible.
- Decentralising power so that smaller units are responsible for a greater number of powers.
- Making clearer the powers of different levels of government.

Local government elections can be abused

A further problem arising from our centralised system is that voters can use local elections to send messages to national government. This can be done at little cost in terms of bad policy at the local level given the relative unimportance of the powers exercised by local government.[3]

---

3   This does suggest rational behaviour on the part of voters.

It does appear that, in practice, local elections are used to punish national governments. For example, in the 1993 county council elections,[4] the ruling Conservative Party lost every single county except for one (Buckinghamshire). However, by 2009,[5] the party controlled all but eight counties in England. These results cannot plausibly reflect the independent performance of county council administrations at these times. During the period of Labour government from 1997 to 2010, there were local elections in most years. In these elections, the Labour Party polled between 7 and 16 percentage points fewer than they did in the previous general election (see Mellows-Facer 2006). There is an almost identical pattern in relation to the Conservative Party between 1979 and 1997.

Overall, this is an extraordinary picture. It suggests either that voters are confusing UK parliamentary election issues with issues relevant to other layers of government or that they are using the other layers of government to register what they believe is a costless mid-term protest against the Westminster government of the day. If local government has few powers, of course, voters may be correct that their actions are costless. However, this picture also suggests that changes of government at the local level will happen almost randomly, as determined by the performance of government at the national level.

---

4   The mid-term of a Conservative government.

5   Towards the end of a Labour government.

The absence of foot voting

While voters are relatively uninformed about political issues, people who migrate from one political jurisdiction to another have a strong incentive to be highly informed about what they are doing. People do not need sophisticated knowledge when moving from one governmental jurisdiction to another – they only need relevant knowledge about whether one area is better than another from their perspective. What Somin (2013) calls 'foot voting' is more effective in disciplining government than ballot box voting. Firstly, those who choose to move area only need to acquire information about the range of things that is directly relevant to the decision. Secondly, there is a much stronger incentive to evaluate that information in a rational and unbiased way given that those making the decision will face the full financial consequences and other consequences of their actions. At the very least, foot voting allows individuals to move from an area where government is performing badly to an area where it is performing better, even if it does not improve the poorly performing government.

We can see that foot voting is practical by observing how parents move home to try to obtain better schools for their children. For example, polling research in the UK suggests that nearly one-third of parents have moved house in England to be in the catchment area for a good school and 10 per cent are willing to pay in excess of an additional £50,000 for a property in a desirable school catchment area.[6] Thus, it is clear that people move to get better services when they are able to do so.

Somin (2013) shows how people have been able to vote with their feet even in the most difficult conditions. However, the structure of the UK government does raise considerable barriers to foot voting being effective. For example, centralisation – often promoted by fears of differences arising between local service provision in different areas of the country or postcode lotteries – leads to greater similarity in service provision across the country.[7] Even where service provision can vary, the fact that spending decisions are often devolved without tax decisions being devolved enables some areas of the UK to spend more per head, effectively financed by other areas of the UK; thus, gains from providing services effectively and efficiently are reduced. Indeed, foot voting can send the wrong signals in the UK system: for example, English voters have an incentive to move to Scotland to receive free long-term care for the elderly or free university tuition financed by the taxpayers of the UK as a whole. The very process of centralisation perhaps breeds a dynamic that causes people to think that services *should be* the same everywhere, even those services nominally controlled by local government.

---

6   http://www.propertywire.com/news/europe/uk-families-move-schools
    -201409099567.html

7   Though there is some difference in school performance (Ofsted 2013) and
    there are also differences in healthcare performance between England and
    the other nations (Bevan et al. 2014).

Of course, foot voting is not a cure-all for bad policy. There are, for example, costs of moving between jurisdictions. However, as Somin (2014) suggests, these costs are not necessarily large relative to the benefits and tend to be lower for the less-well-off, who do not own property. The decentralisation proposed below will tend to lower the costs of foot voting – there is no pretence that they can be reduced to zero. It is also frequently suggested that there can be a race to the bottom as a result of local areas lowering taxes to attract population or to reduce the likelihood that citizens will move. However, this is unlikely. If services are efficiently provided and of value to local citizens they will have no reason to move. People do not move on the basis of tax rates alone – as has been noted above in relation to schooling. Sometimes a jurisdiction might lower taxes on mobile factors of production and raise them on immobile factors of production, thereby exploiting the ability of different factors of production to vote with their feet. However, that is less likely given the constraints on the shape of the tax base proposed below.

Other disadvantages of fiscal centralisation

If spending is decentralised without taxation being decentralised, the ability of a local authority to grow its tax base by following good policy is reduced. More generally, as Sinclair (2014) argues, if local governments do not raise their own revenue, they have no incentive to grow their tax base by following policies that are favourable to business and attractive to the local population. Innovation can also be reduced in centralised systems. And if grants are ring-fenced by government and have to be used for specific purposes, there is very limited scope for experimentation. These problems can be exacerbated where central government allocates grants according to complex formulae which may, in fact, benefit local authorities that are in population decline or in economic and social decline. Indeed, as we shall suggest below, decentralisation of spending combined with centralised revenue raising may produce the worst results.

Blöchliger (2013: 8–9) argues that decentralisation leads to two main benefits. It will increase the productivity of all government spending because mobile factors of production (foot voters) can discipline local government. Furthermore, the spending that does take place is likely to be on more important services that are valued by businesses and residents. Local authorities can experiment and other local authorities can copy policies that work.

Tax decentralisation also allows local authorities to choose a tax and charging mix that is more closely aligned to providing appropriate public goods within the relevant area. For example, a tourist tax on hotel occupants, if carefully spent and not set at levels that are too high, can both offset the costs tourists impose on an area and help pay for public goods related to tourism (maps, tourist information centres, hill paths, clean beaches and so on), which it might not be feasible to finance through direct charges.

In a more decentralised political system it is not only residents who are able to compare local services and taxes, politicians can do so too when holding administrators to account (see Tullock 1976). In general, politicians may be less responsive to voters than businesses are to consumers; however, they do have an incentive to provide better services at a given cost. With more local government responsibility, politicians (as well as voters and residents) can compare outcomes in different parts of the country with a view to more effectively holding to account the bureaucracy that is delivering the services.

As Tullock also points out, fiscal decentralisation makes logrolling (or, more generally, the problem of a small number of voters imposing upon all voters increased taxes to finance spending that benefits relatively few people) more difficult. If a particular city, such as Manchester, wishes to improve infrastructure, build museums and theatres or new schools and hospitals, and so on, at taxpayer expense, under a decentralised political system it would be the taxpayers of Manchester who would bear the cost. The voters of Manchester would not be able to benefit from these things while imposing the costs on the taxpayers of the country as a whole – they would have to bear the costs themselves.

Benefits of fiscal decentralisation – the evidence

There is a significant amount of evidence that fiscal decentralisation increases economic performance over a range of indicators. For example, Blöchliger (2013) finds that fiscal decentralisation is associated with higher national income, better school performance and higher levels of investment (both physical investment and investment in human capital). In particular, he finds, consistent with Ashworth et al. (2013) (see below), that the decentralisation of revenue-raising powers has a stronger effect on performance than the decentralisation of spending.

The effects of decentralisation are strong. Blöchliger (2013: 3) finds that:

> Doubling sub-central tax or spending shares (e.g. increasing the ratio of sub-central to general government tax revenue from 6 to 12%) is associated with a GDP per capita increase of around 3%.

It should be noted that it cannot be assumed that a huge step change in a particular country would replicate this result. However, UK sub-central tax revenue is less than half of that in France and only one-tenth of that in Canada, so this does suggest substantial benefits from decentralisation. Overall, taking into account the fact that the relationship between decentralisation and economic performance is non-linear, Blöchliger suggests that, if the UK raised the same proportion of tax revenue at sub-national level as Sweden, it would increase national income by 4 per cent. However, the most significant gains would come from the initial reductions in the proportion of revenue raised centrally.

There is a great deal of other evidence on the benefits of decentralisation and the Lyons report into local government financing (Lyons 2007: Executive Summary 33) concluded:

Recent work comparing the UK with the USA and Europe has concluded that the lack of devolution and local discretion in the UK is a constraint on economic performance, particularly in the cities.

Nevertheless, the picture is not completely straightforward. Ashworth et al. (2013) have studied the impact of spending localisation and tax localisation on the size of government. They find that the decentralisation of spending tends to lead to bigger government – that is higher government spending. On the other hand, decentralisation of taxation can lead to smaller government.

This conclusion is consistent with other studies. For example, work by the IMF (specifically, Cottarelli 2009) confirms the above results while making the additional point that it is important for fiscal discipline to be maintained in the sub-national government areas (through fiscal rules or credible no-bailout mechanisms, which ensure that sub-national governments can go bankrupt). Furthermore, it is also important that local government has the administrative capacity to raise and spend revenue.

Overall, the evidence would suggest that decentralisation would help economic performance, especially if the focus were on revenue raising with fiscal discipline being maintained.

But, does fiscal decentralisation lead to a race to the bottom with local governments that fear voter migration due to high taxes providing inadequate services? There is, in fact, no reason to assume there would be a race to the bottom if local authorities have more revenue-raising and spending powers. While local authorities may compete to have lower tax rates and provide fewer services, as Tiebout (1956) points out, many of the services that local government provides have 'public good' characteristics. It might be the case that such services would be better provided by the private sector but, insofar as this is not the case, businesses and residents are likely to prefer the best package of services and revenue raising rather than the smallest package of services. Of course, residents would also prefer a given package of services to be provided at the lowest cost. The incentives are more likely to be aligned with the achievement of this objective if both tax raising and service provision take place at a local level. Blöchliger and Campos (2011) confirm this result, arguing that 'a race to the bottom cannot be observed.'

In common with the studies cited above, Thießen (2003) finds that fiscal decentralisation is growth promoting. However, when fiscal decentralisation reaches high levels, it can reduce growth. Indeed, it is clear that there must come a point when some public goods are more efficiently provided on a national scale, so this result is not surprising.

More generally, the evidence regarding fiscal decentralisation is not all in one direction. It is possible that fiscal decentralisation has a detrimental impact on economic performance in certain circumstances. For example, if a country has weak institutions and high levels of corruption, it might be difficult to envisage such a country having the capacity to govern effectively at local level – though, on the other hand, it may be possible for local government in some areas to bypass the problems caused by weak institutions in the country as a whole. In the UK in the 1970s and 1980s, an extremely narrow tax base might well have contributed to the poor performance of local government in some areas. Also, we might expect small countries to benefit less from fiscal decentralisation, given that the optimal scale on which public goods can be provided might then be closer to the population of the country as a whole.

Rodriguez-Pose and Ezcurra (2011) suggest that fiscal decentralisation has had a negative impact on growth across 21 OECD countries. However, while the results of this research should lead us to question whether fiscal decentralisation is always and everywhere a good thing, two shortcomings make it less relevant to the UK case. Firstly, Rodriguez-Pose and Ezcurra examine the impact of fiscal decentralisation on growth and not on national income levels. It is unclear why decentralisation would necessarily affect growth – changes in decentralisation might lead to changes in national income (and therefore growth in the short term) but decentralisation itself is likely to lead to a higher level of income rather than a higher growth path. Secondly, they did not adjust for country size (because country size was strongly correlated with the level of fiscal decentralisation).

The benefits of reform in the UK

In a sense, the more nuanced results should lead us to be even more emphatic about the conclusions for the UK. The UK is in the worst position possible. It has very low levels of fiscal decentralisation, and tax raising is much more centralised than spending. Overall, the evidence suggests that it would not be possible to devise a more damaging combination. Secondly, the UK is a large country in which it would be expected to efficiently provide public goods at a sub-national level. Thirdly, migration within the UK is substantial but migration from the UK to other countries is difficult because of either language difficulties (in the case of EU countries) or immigration restrictions (in the case of English-speaking countries). As such, starting from the current position, with relatively high levels of local spending financed by grants, devolving revenue raising to the local level should lead to much better outcomes

4 INTERNATIONAL EXPERIENCE: THE EXAMPLE OF SPAIN

It is not the purpose of this paper to provide a comprehensive set of case studies from overseas. The general empirical evidence has already been examined. However, any empirical study using aggregate data can hide very specific features that can determine the success (or otherwise) of fiscal decentralisation. In this section, we consider the case of Spain, which would appear to demonstrate that fiscal decentralisation needs to be handled carefully if it is to be successful.

Spain has had increasing levels of devolution to regional governments (*comunidades autónomas* or 'autonomous communities' – ACs) since 1978.

Progressive devolution with asymmetries

For much of the last two centuries, Spain was a heavily centralised country. There were brief yet repeated attempts at decentralisation throughout this period, one of which started during the Second Republic from 1931, but was cut short by the Civil War of 1936–39 and then decisively reversed by the Franco dictatorship, which lasted until 1975 (Heywood 2000).

As part of the constitutional process during Spain's transition to democracy from the mid-1970s, the constitution's framers sought to accommodate the demands for greater autonomy by nationalist sectors in a number of regions. The rationale was that, since these regions – which included the Basque Country, Catalonia and Galicia – had a history of self-government and salient independent identities, they should be granted autonomy over the management of a large number of regional affairs (Ruiz Almendral 2012). This had to be achieved while retaining the equal treatment of all Spanish citizens.

The solution offered has become known as Spain's 'State of the Autonomies' (*Estado de las Autonomías*). At the heart of the system was a process of asymmetric decentralisation of powers to the ACs. Such asymmetry took two forms. Firstly, it transferred competencies to different regions at different paces between 1979 and 2002, when the process was completed.[1] Secondly, it gave two ACs, the Basque Country and Navarre, special tax-raising powers in recognition of their historical rights guaranteed by royal charters (*fueros*) over the centuries (Fernández Llera 2009). All other fifteen ACs were granted much more limited revenue-raising powers.

Progressive devolution of spending over the last four decades has radically transformed the structure of public administration in Spain. As Table 4 illustrates, between 1982 and 2008 the share of total public spending disbursed

---

1   Power transfers in each AC followed one of three routes prescribed in the 1978 Spanish Constitution. Heywood (2000) explains the process in greater detail.

Table 4   Local, regional and national government spending as a
percentage of total Spanish public expenditure

	1982	1995	2008	2013
Local government	10.6	11.1	13.3	10.8
Autonomous Communities (ACs)	3.6	21.5	36.5	31.6
Central government (incl. Social Security)	85.5	67.3	50.2	57.6

Source: Cuenca (2009); Intervención General de la Administración del Estado; OECD Fiscal Decentralisation Database (2015). Figures are approximate and may not add up to 100 per cent.

by ACs grew tenfold, while central government's share dropped from 85 per cent to just over half the total.

The growth in ACs' share of public spending reflects the gradual transfer of responsibility from the central government to the ACs for the management of a large array of government programmes, notably healthcare, education, employment and environmental policy. In many of these areas, the national government has retained prerogatives to set the general framework of policy, while ACs are tasked with implementation (Heywood 2000). At the same time, the central government maintains full control over areas seen as being of national importance, including not just defence and foreign relations but also taxation collection, public works and road and train networks involving more than one AC, as well as some large ports and airports.

While spending has been substantially decentralised since 1978, revenue-raising responsibilities have not been decentralised to the same degree. As Table 5 shows, ACs' share of tax revenue has lagged behind by as much as 13 percentage points compared with their share of total

Table 5   Local, regional and national tax revenue as a
            percentage of total tax revenue in Spain

	1982	1995	2008	2013
Local government	7.5	8.5	9.6	10.1
Autonomous Communities (ACs)	1.5	4.8	23.8	25.4
Central government (incl. Social Security)	91.0	86.7	68.4	64.6

Source: OECD Fiscal Decentralisation Database (2015). Figures are approximate and may
not add up to 100 per cent.

government spending. Even this overstates AC's tax autonomy, since much of their revenue comes from so-called ceded
taxes – such as a share of personal income tax and VAT, as
well as inheritance and gift tax, wealth tax, gambling taxes
and other taxes – which are, to a large extent, determined
by the central government.[2] ACs have some limited control
over rate setting and deductions, but they have to follow the
general framework set by the national government.

Ignoring the issue of ceded taxes, however, it is worth
noting that Spain is much more decentralised than the UK,
both from the revenue point of view and from the point of
view of the amount of spending controlled by sub-central
government.

Nevertheless, despite enjoying significant powers over
the allocation and management of public spending, ACs
are heavily dependent on the central government to finance their outlays (Ruiz Almendral 2002, 2004). Their
main sources of income are thus revenue from the ceded

2   This has led some scholars (Ruiz Almendral 2002; Heywood 2000) to view
    ceded taxes more as central government transfers than own sources of AC
    tax revenue.

taxes, as well as conditional and unconditional transfers from the national government.[3] Transfers are determined through a complex formula (see de la Fuente 2012) taking into account expected and real tax revenue from the AC in question, which is then adjusted for factors that may warrant additional funding (e.g. regional languages, low density and scattered populations). The final figure for each region is arrived at through regular political negotiations between AC governments and the central government on a bilateral and multilateral basis.

The details of the system are beyond the scope of this chapter, but it becomes clear that there is an acute imbalance between ACs' tax and spending powers. Successive reforms were passed in 1997, 2002 and 2009 to try to close the gap (de la Fuente 2012), and while some progress has been made the tax autonomy of regional governments remains limited.

Problems with Spain's devolution settlement

The most salient problem with Spain's current system of devolution is that it lacks incentives for ACs to manage their affairs efficiently. As Ruiz Almendral (2004) has pointed out, the status quo enables regional governments to make spending decisions without having to account for the required tax revenue, and without having to explain to voters why such spending is necessary and worth the cost.

---

3   There has been a third major source of income for some ACs in the form of EU structural funds since Spain joined the European Community in 1986.

What is more, to the extent that increased expenditures can be used as an argument for additional central government transfers in budget negotiations, regional politicians are encouraged to live above their means. In addition, a bargaining process with central government has replaced representation of the local electorate as the main way in which resources are allocated – somewhat similar to the situation with the devolved nations within the UK.

These incentives appear to have borne the fruit that would be expected. Even in the boom years that preceded the 2008 crash, when the central government was posting budget surpluses of up to 2 per cent of GDP, the ACs had difficulty managing their books (Cuenca 2009). While there was strong variation across regions, most AC governments – with the notable exception of the Basque Country and Navarre, which operate under a more balanced and decentralised regime – recorded small deficits. Many administrations spent lavishly on items of questionable value, such as regional public broadcasters, remote airports and myriad cultural facilities (*The Economist* 2008). It is telling that AC government-owned enterprises saw their debts grow more than fourfold between 1995 and 2007, compared with 50 per cent for all state-owned enterprises (Fernández Llera 2009).

The economic crisis that gripped Spain between 2008 and 2013 further highlighted the deficiencies of the system. AC budget deficits soared across the board, reaching levels of up to 6 per cent (Cuenca 2009). Given the acuteness of the downturn, the rapid rise in regional government budget shortfalls cannot solely be blamed on a poor devolution settlement, but it was arguably made worse by it. More importantly, the ACs' lack of own resources to meet their spending commitments pushed the government to take increasing responsibility over the design and management of regional budgets. In a process akin to developments taking place in the euro zone around the same time, central authorities attempted to set strict deficit and debt targets for ACs to follow, with limited success (Cuenca 2009; Ruiz Almendral and Cuenca 2014). This undermined a fundamental principle underlying the devolved constitutional settlement in Spain, namely that regional governments enjoy autonomy over the management of their financial affairs. It also decisively hurt the credibility of the no-bailout principle (which had never been explicitly acknowledged), raising concerns about moral hazard and the probability that the ACs would expect central government assistance in future budget crises.

Lessons for the UK

Prior to the crisis, the devolution settlement in Spain was widely viewed as broadly successful, if still a work in progress (Heywood 2000; Ruiz Almendral 2002). The 2008 downturn exposed the severe weaknesses in the system, which stemmed largely from a persistent lack of revenue-raising responsibilities to match the ACs' spending powers together with no effective mechanisms to ensure fiscal responsibility. Reforms aimed at increasing regional governments' tax autonomy addressed the imbalance only mildly, and they failed to introduce adequate incentives for ACs to take responsibility over their spending commitments. This not only undermined the principles underlying devolution, but also compromised the soundness of Spain's public finances at all levels of government.

The experience of the crisis together with renewed pressures for self-government in Catalonia and (to a lesser degree) the Basque Country pushed policymakers to recognise the need for substantial reform by way of genuine fiscal decentralisation. This could follow the model of the Basque Country and Navarre, which, due to their *foral* status, have responsibility for raising the vast majority of taxes, including personal income tax, corporation tax and VAT. In turn, they transfer a small amount (*cupo*) to the central government to pay for nationally provided services.[4] This means that they are self-reliant for over 90 per cent of their expenditures and receive less than 3 per cent of their resources from the central government (Ruiz Almendral 2004). Extending the arrangements in these two ACs to all other regions would turn Spain into a genuinely federal country, more akin to Germany or Canada.

The Spanish experience offers three key lessons for any future process of devolution in the UK.

Firstly, any arrangement that does not couple the transfer of spending responsibilities with a concomitant decentralisation of tax-raising powers will make the system fragile and undermine governance. The UK has

---

4   There has been some controversy over the specific amount to be transferred to the national government, with some observers claiming it is too low compared with the services provided in exchange. Nevertheless, it is the arrangement itself rather than the figures that matter for our analysis.

already made that mistake and it led to fragility and instability. The decentralisation of tax raising powers should also be explicit, as, for example, in Canada. This ensures that the important relationships are between the elected representatives and the people rather than the elected representatives and the federal government.

Secondly, there must be an *explicit* no-bailout principle that is stated from the outset. This would apply to both national governments within the UK (such as Scotland) and local government. Only in this way can accountability and fiscal responsibility be ensured. Canada has a very clear no-bailout tradition and provinces have in the past been allowed to default and take the consequences.[5] This alone does not necessarily stop a sub-federal entity building up debt,[6] but it should help, especially when combined with constitutional restrictions on borrowing, and it also makes clear where fiscal responsibility lies.

Thirdly, the settlement should be symmetrical: regions, nations or local authorities should not have different degrees of decentralised powers while at the same time having the same representation in parliament.

---

5   http://www.conferenceboard.ca/economics/hot_eco_topics/default/ 11-11-30/provincial_debt_is_not_a_federal_responsibility.aspx

6   See Speer (2014) for a discussion of Quebec's debt position.

5   DEALING WITH THE ENGLISH QUESTION: HALF-BAKED SOLUTIONS

As has already been noted, the problems posed by devolution are not new to the UK. Precisely the problems described above existed in relation to Northern Ireland until direct rule was established in 1972 and they were anticipated in the discussions surrounding home rule for Ireland in the late nineteenth and early twentieth centuries (see Bowers 2012). For example, when home rule for Ireland was discussed, proposals included the exclusion of Irish members from the House of Commons, reducing the number of Irish members or preventing them from voting on issues that were decided in Ireland (the equivalent to English votes for English laws, which is being discussed in parliament at the time of writing). Rather later, when, in the event, Northern Ireland was given devolved powers, the number of Northern Irish MPs was reduced. Translated into the current conjuncture, however, none of these solutions is satisfactory.

English votes for English laws (EVEL)

If members of parliament in the nations with devolved government were excluded from the UK parliament altogether

– as was suggested in the case of Irish home rule – it would mean that they could not vote on matters to do with the taxes that would be raised in their constituencies to pay for UK-wide or devolved spending. It would also mean that they could not vote on matters pertaining to the UK as a whole. This is clearly unsatisfactory and is not under serious consideration. An alternative to this approach would be to exclude non-English members of parliament from votes relating to measures that only affect England. However, there are several problems with this proposal, which has become known as 'English votes for English laws' (EVEL).

EVEL would, in effect, mean that in some circumstances, depending on the outcome of a general election, a stable government could not be formed that could propose legislation on and administer departments in relation to all issues. For example, there could be a Labour government in the UK as a whole, dealing with matters such as foreign affairs and proposing budgets. At the same time, that government might not be able to legislate in England on areas related to health and education, on which Scottish members would have no vote.

Packer and Sinclair (2015) also point out that this so-called EVEL proposal would weaken accountability. It would mean that some MPs were responsible for two sets of issues and others only one. It would be very difficult to identify the executive that was responsible for English issues. If there were dissatisfaction with the health service, for example, would that be the fault of the relevant ministry, the organisation of the service in England or the financing of the service through the Treasury? The whole system would be very confusing.

This problem could be avoided by creating an entirely separate English parliament, but this would create yet another level of government (also see Packer and Sinclair, 2015). Some English electors are already represented at parish or town, district, county, UK and EU level and this proposal would create a sixth level of representation.[1]

Reducing the number of non-English members of parliament

Reducing the number of non-English members of parliament would help dilute the problem of non-English members being able to vote on matters that do not affect their constituents, but would not solve it.[2] Furthermore, this would create other anomalies. If this policy were followed, non-English members would be under-represented on those matters that pertained to the whole of the UK (for example, defence and foreign policy) while still being able to vote on issues that did not affect their constituents, such as health and education, albeit in smaller numbers.

---

1 Though the federal system proposed below would also have an additional level of representation, the delineation of powers would be very clear and the powers of the federal parliament very limited.

2 Harold Wilson expressed concern about the potentially decisive votes of the Ulster Unionist Party in the 1964 parliament when they were voting on issues that had been devolved to Northern Ireland. In that case there were only a handful of Northern Ireland members who could have swayed the result of a vote.

Devolution within England

A further possibility would be to devolve more power to local government in England. This is proposed by Packer and Sinclair (2015). Their proposal is not so much half-baked as an incomplete solution that needs to be complemented by other measures. A different approach that involves moving to regional government, on the other hand, would bring with it a number of problems.

Decentralisation to local government

Decentralisation as proposed by Packer and Sinclair would be welcome. Indeed, it is proposed below, together with a new settlement for the nations within the UK. In theory, if everything that is being devolved in Scotland were also devolved to English local authority areas, then this would resolve the West Lothian question and the other problems with the current settlement that are discussed above. However, following this approach without complementary reforms throws up some major problems. Firstly, the median population of the main local government areas in England is around 250,000. Packer and Sinclair rightly say that this is no smaller than similar local government units in other countries that have much more decentralised systems. Nevertheless, the amount of devolution to Scotland (and arguably Northern Ireland and Wales) would then be constrained by the amount of feasible decentralisation to local government. Secondly, Scotland has its own traditions and cultures, which may make it appropriate to devolve more aspects of economic and political decision-making to that nation. Limiting the extent of devolution to Scotland would prevent the beneficial competition between and experimentation within Scotland and England on the very broad range of issues that could come under each nation's government.

Devolution to the regions

A different approach to devolution within England would involve giving powers to the regions. This issue was raised by the dissenters to the Royal Commission on the Constitution published in 1973.[3] They believed that it was wrong to give devolved powers to Scotland and Wales without a symmetrical devolution settlement to ensure that Scottish and Welsh members of the UK parliament were not voting on issues that only affected England – in other words, they articulated exactly the same concerns as those discussed above. Their proposal was to create English regions with similar powers to those of any Scottish and Welsh government that might be created.

Such proposals have a certain logic to them. When devolution was implemented in 1999, the government attempted to create regional assemblies in England to complement the Scottish parliament and Welsh assembly. However, there are a number of problems with this approach. Firstly, there is little enthusiasm for it within

---

3   The dissenters were Professor Alan Peacock and Lord Crowther-Hunt; the report is known as the Kilbrandon Report.

England. Only 11 per cent of the North East's electorate voted in favour of an elected regional assembly in a referendum held in 2004 – and this region was regarded as being the one most likely to be enthusiastic about a regional assembly. Secondly, unless regions took over all the functions of the proposed RUK (or English, Welsh and Northern Irish) parliaments, there would be an extra layer of government needed. Thirdly, there is no distinct legal system or any other feature of English regions, which would seem to point in the direction of autonomy. Regions also do not even have established boundaries. Furthermore, a regional devolution settlement would make it much harder to resist the pull to the centre that arises in federal systems. For example, a federal country of around ten regional entities could less easily operate on the principle of unanimity.

Overall, a regional devolution settlement that was radical enough to deal with the English question would essentially be constructivist – that is, it would involve the entire remodelling of the British constitution around a unit of government that was arbitrary from both the political and the geographical points of view. Certainly, it could be argued that current local authority areas should be merged, broken up or changed because their creation in the past was also arbitrary, but that is an entirely different argument. The federalist and localist solutions proposed below, on the other hand, involve a natural evolution of current arrangements together with a return of powers to entities from which they have been centralised in the first place.

6 A FEDERAL SOLUTION TO THE ENGLISH PROBLEM

The most appropriate system of governance for the UK is an entirely federal solution. It has none of the faults of the other proposals and many advantages.

In order to implement this proposal there would have to be a parliamentary act proposing that referenda should be held in Scotland, England, Wales and Northern Ireland. The referenda could pose alternatives such as the status quo or full independence for Scotland and the other nations. However, the main proposal would be for a federal system to be created. Within that federal system, Wales and Northern Ireland would have to decide whether they should be independent nations in the same way as Scotland or join England while having a degree of devolution.

For ease of exposition, we propose that the basic governmental units should become Scotland and the Rest of the UK (RUK).

Functions of the federal government

Although an indication of the powers that would be held at federal and national levels would have to be given at the time of the referenda, there would be an opportunity to change these by unanimous agreement at a later time. Ideally, the federal functions would be limited to:

- defence
- border control (and, by implication, migration and the consequential potential financial costs in relation to the financing of asylum seekers and refugees[1])
- foreign affairs (including issues related to EU membership and, hence, trade)
- the management of the existing national debt
- possibly, monetary affairs and banking regulation, assuming that both countries wished to keep a central bank[2]

It is assumed that all UK nations would share the same head of state. Policy related to offshore and onshore national resources would be a function of the national governments (Scotland and RUK) rather than the federal government, though there are proposals below to further localise the regulation of onshore natural resources (such as fracked natural gas).

What is the rationale for these powers being maintained by the federal government? Ricketts (2004) discusses the

---

1   As it happens, there might be considerable benefits in completely decoupling the financial costs of looking after asylum seekers and refugees from the welfare system designed for people who are permanently resident.

2   This would be an opportunity to try alternative monetary arrangements such as proposed by Hayek (1990). Such arrangements served Scotland well in the late eighteenth and early nineteenth centuries.

competencies of the EU and notes how far they have deviated from those which economic analysis would suggest that the EU should have. For example, EU-wide public goods such as defence are not provided at the EU level, while many functions of the EU, such as the management of fisheries, could be more efficiently provided by nation states or by markets. If we believe that one of the most important functions of government is the provision of public goods that cannot necessarily be provided by the market,[3] then it is reasonable to provide at federal level those public goods for which there are likely to be considerable scale economies at the federal level or for which there are significant externalities or spillovers if the services were provided at nation state or local level.

Of course, without a market for such services and a process of competitive discovery (see Kirzner 1992), it is impossible to know on what scale public goods should be provided. Nevertheless, judgements do have to be made about how to distribute powers in a federal system. On balance, it would not seem unreasonable that, in the case of an island,[4] defence, border control and foreign affairs would be best managed at the federal level. It would also seem logical to manage the historically accumulated national debt at federal level given that it was accumulated under a unitary UK government.

---

3   This paper discusses the reform of the UK constitution and it is not our intention to discuss at length whether many so-called public goods are, in fact, club goods that could be provided by the market. Whichever layer of government is responsible for a particular area of policy could, if it wished, open up provision to the market or to civil society groups.

4   Though, of course, Northern Ireland is not part of mainland Britain.

Should environmental problems be handled at the federal level?

There will, of course, be other issues that it might be sensible to deal with at the federal level. These may include environmental problems that involve cross-border externalities or dealing with the breakout of communicable diseases in farm animals. The functions to be performed at federal level can be changed using the processes outlined. However, it should not be thought that all areas of policy that involve these kinds of externalities need to be handled at the federal level. To begin with, the EU has a very significant role here.[5] Under the Lisbon Treaty, the environment is a joint EU/member state competence and there are few major environmental issues where EU policy would not drive policy in the UK. For example, the foot and mouth disease outbreak in 2001 was handled administratively by the relevant UK government department, but policy discretion was severely limited by EU directives.

Where there are cross-border environmental issues that are not under the influence of EU policy, intergovernmental cooperation within the federation may well be the most appropriate solution. (This is the approach, for example, that is taken with regard to the Rhine, which flows through several countries and is protected by the Convention on the Protection of the Rhine, which is

---

5 No judgement is made in this paper about whether these roles are correctly defined.

signed by the EU and five Rhine-bordering countries.) However, there may still be a potentially very small number of issues that are not under the authority of the EU and where cooperation between the nations within a federal UK might not be feasible because just one of the UK nations is imposing costs upon another and has no incentive to cooperate. This is, though, no different from the position that pertains in relation to any other set of EU countries that share land borders, including the UK and the Republic of Ireland.

Monetary affairs and banking regulation

Monetary policy is also complex. Debates over monetary affairs were at the heart of the recent Scottish independence referendum. Monetary policy could be handled in many ways: Scotland and RUK could have separate central banks; the current arrangement could be maintained and be the responsibility of the federal government; the central bank could be maintained in England but with Scotland establishing a currency board; or either constituent nation could choose to abolish central banks altogether.

The author's preference is for one of the latter two solutions (preferably the last). However, if central banks are maintained, it is important for banking regulation to be undertaken on a consistent basis with central banking functions. If central banking is a federal responsibility, then banking regulation should be also.

One argument in favour of keeping central banking as a federal responsibility is that the banking systems of Scotland and RUK are so closely integrated, and will remain so as long as the UK remains part of the EU, that establishing separate central banking and monetary systems would be costly. A second argument is that the UK is likely to be potentially much closer to an optimal currency area than euro zone countries are, and that the sharing of a currency reduces transactions costs. Against this, some would maintain that, given that it is being proposed that the federal government has no competency in the field of redistribution or other fiscal transfers, Scotland and RUK might be less resilient in the face of specific shocks that affect one part of the federation. Such an argument has been made by those who believe that European monetary union should go hand in hand with greater fiscal responsibilities for the EU layer of government.[6]

On balance, the author proposes keeping monetary affairs and banking regulation as a federal responsibility, but this would be one of the areas that might generate greatest debate and subsequent reform. The onus would be on the Scottish and RUK governments to ensure that their economies were sufficiently deregulated at the microeconomic level so that macroeconomic shocks would not have sustainable impacts on employment.[7]

---

6   For example, this was recently proposed by the French president, François Hollande (http://openeurope.org.uk/blog/hollande-proposes-a-eurozone -government/) and is widely discussed by economists.

7   Again, this has been widely discussed in the case of the euro. See, for example, http://www.cer.org.uk/in-the-press/euros-success-requires-liberalisation

Functions of national (Scottish and RUK) governments

All other major government functions would be the ultimate responsibility of the national governments within the UK (assumed to be Scotland and RUK). This does not mean that such functions should be centralised within and controlled by national governments. On the one hand, action will be circumscribed by international treaties: UK membership of the EU and the World Trade Organization, for example, would prevent the Scottish or RUK governments from imposing trade barriers. On the other hand, there should be significant decentralisation of government functions as discussed below. However, in areas such as policing, health, education, policy in relation to natural resources (both offshore and onshore), welfare and pensions, criminal, civil and commercial law, the provision of foreign aid, arts policy, the environment and land-use planning, there would be no federal responsibility – simply intergovernmental cooperation if that were desired. Government intervention could then only take place if desired by the Scottish or RUK governments within their own jurisdictions.

A further function that would generally be handled by the Scottish and RUK governments acting separately would be legal issues relating to personal freedoms and, where appropriate, human rights. This is an area of some difficulty as the UK does not have a written constitution. Fundamental rights are currently protected through a range of mechanisms (international treaties, statute law, common law and so on). International obligations (such as the European Convention on Human Rights) would remain and therefore be in force throughout the whole of the UK. There may be some issues which, as a result of other competences being exercised at the federal level, might be handled by the federal government. These could include the treatment and finance of provision for asylum seekers, for example. However, issues such as abortion, hunting, laws relating to marriage and to euthanasia should be competences for Scotland and RUK separately. Scotland already has its own legal system and competence over some of these matters and, indeed, even Northern Ireland has separate legislation in relation to abortion. Dealing with such matters at the lower level of government rather than at the federal level allows laws to take account of the preferences and cultures of the nations concerned while also allowing foot voting by those who might prefer alternative policies.

Synchronising economics and politics

It might be argued that there are wider political considerations that should be taken into account when assigning functions to different levels of government. Indeed, Bastable, writing on public finance from an economic point of view back in 1895, pointed out that the structure of government is often determined by historical evolution. It is not the purpose of this economic analysis to engage with that debate directly. However, it is worth noting that for most of the period for which the Union has existed (1707 until at least 1914) government was limited in its functions to defence, foreign affairs, the regulation of trade (which has effectively become an EU function), monetary policy (for part of the period) and the management of the national debt. Governments in the UK did little else. As such, distinct Scottish and English (and sometimes Northern Irish and Welsh) traditions developed in areas such as education, law and criminal justice and the provision of social insurances. Progressively, policy was centralised under the UK government, but that period of centralisation was relatively brief and began to reverse in 1999. Sometimes these different traditions have been based on distinct policies being followed in the different nations within the UK, and sometimes through the development of independent welfare institutions within the various countries of the UK. The important point is that there is a significant similarity between the functions proposed for the federal government and those for which the UK government was responsible from 1707 to 1914. Those functions that it is proposed are removed from the domain of the federal UK government have only been functions of a centralised British state for a short period of time. Thus, the economic analysis of the functions that should be handled centrally by a federal government would seem to run with the grain of history.

Federal, UK and Scottish parliaments

Both a Scottish parliament and an RUK parliament would be established to deal with matters that were not UK-wide. In addition, there would be a UK parliament that could be small and meet infrequently except during times of national emergency. It is not the purpose of this paper to discuss exactly how the parliaments would be elected, but there would be a stronger case for fixed terms and a much smaller number of members in the UK-wide parliament. It would also not be unreasonable for the smaller nations to be over-represented compared with their populations in the federal parliament. For illustration, a possible set of arrangements for the various parliaments is shown in Box 1.

Preventing re-centralisation of power

A proper federal solution should put the power in the hands of Scotland and RUK to devolve power upwards to the federal union, rather than the authority for determining

---

Box 1   Possible political arrangements for a federal UK

Federal parliament

- Maximum term – five years.
- One hundred members of the federal parliament, determined in the following way: five for Northern Ireland; five for Wales; ten for Scotland; twenty for England; the rest determined by population.
- All members of parliament to be elected by first-past-the-post or alternative vote with roughly equal constituency populations within each home nation.

- Second chamber with forty members elected for a maximum of one ten-year term with strictly no institutional party campaign finance or backing, and ten hereditary members elected by the current hereditary peers. The sole function of this chamber would be to be propose amendments to or return for reconsideration legislation of the first chamber.
- Five government departments.
- No more than fifteen government ministers, limited by statute.
- Ministers could be drawn from either house of parliament.
- Members of both chambers would sit for one week per month during ten months of the year.

RUK parliament

- Maximum term – five years.
- Four hundred members of parliament in constituencies of roughly equal population to be elected by first-past-the-post or alternative vote.
- Five government departments plus a Department of Federal Affairs to deal with the interface between federal and national issues.
- Maximum of twenty ministers limited by statute.
- Ministers could be drawn from outside parliament.
- Members of parliament, but not ministers, would be part-time – roughly 30 hours a week.

which powers lie where being held at the federal level. Many federal unions or international bodies made up of nation states have seen a centralisation of power at the federal or supranational level. This has happened within the EU and also within the US. Both Bolick (1994) and Vaubel (2009) argue that institutional design is the key to preventing centralisation.

In any system that works on the basis of majorities and has federal institutions that favour centralisation, there tends to be an accretion of powers to the centre; once they lie with the centre, these powers are difficult to return to the federal units (or member states in the case of the EU). Constitutional protections are often not effective if the constitutional court is at the federal/supranational level because, where issues require interpretation, which is normally the case, the constitutional court tends to favour authority being moved to the higher level of government. The solution to this problem (proposed in different ways and in somewhat different contexts by both Bolick and Vaubel) is to require unanimity at the sub-federal level when decisions are taken about where powers should lie.

This principle, while difficult to implement in a 50- or 28-state union, is much easier to implement in the federal system proposed here. It is proposed that, for any competence to be passed upwards to the UK level, there would have to be agreement in each of the Scottish, RUK and UK parliaments. There would also have to be agreement from the Scottish, RUK and federal parliaments for powers to be passed down from the UK level. Unanimity – which is essential in any federal system to prevent the drift to centralisation – would be realistic and practical in the UK context.

Centralisation also tends to arise where there are ambiguous clauses in constitutions which are interpreted in a centralising way by federal institutions that hold the ultimate power. Bolick cites the interstate commerce clause in the US constitution as being important in promoting centralisation. And the same can be argued in relation to the development of the EU single market; this evolved from the promotion of trade based on mutual recognition of national regulations to the harmonisation of regulation at EU level (see Booth and Morrison 2012). The fundamental problem is that, once the federal level is given power to regulate trade (to prevent trade barriers developing within the country), almost any form of regulation at the central level can be justified because of its relevance to promoting trade.

There is no straightforward solution to this problem. However, as long as the UK remains part of the EU, nearly all such trade-related issues will be handled at the EU level, and thus the problem might be relatively limited in practice. Indeed, unless the UK leaves the EU, it would not be necessary for powers in relation to trade regulation to be delineated at all.

There are various other details that would need to be worked out and which are not discussed further here. For example, there would inevitably be some areas over which the federal and national governments might claim sovereignty (or a legitimate interest), e.g. a major public or animal health crisis close to borders. Would it be the federal government or the national governments that would determine whether or not animal movements had to cease? The small number of nations involved should make conflict less problematic, but there would need to be a constitutional court that would determine whether an issue was a matter for the individual nations or a federal matter, and whether a matter would require dual authority, so that a lower-level parliament could veto the federal government.

Ensuring no bailouts

A second problem with federal systems is the treatment of government borrowing at the sub-federal level. This must be dealt with very clearly ex ante and the following principles would be sustainable and provide the right incentives for sound fiscal management:

- The existing UK-wide debt would remain and be managed by the UK government. Taxes would be levied to service this and/or pay it down as appropriate.
- The UK-wide government could increase its debt level from that inherited at the outset of the federal structure (measured as a proportion of national income) but only with the agreement of UK, Scottish and RUK parliaments.
- Only UK-wide debt would be acceptable for monetary policy operations of the central bank if the central bank were to operate across the UK.

- There would be strictly no bailout of the debts of RUK or Scotland and all debt issued by those governments would be on that understanding.[8]

It is not the purpose of this paper to lay out in detail how the budgets of the constituent parts of government will look. However, we might expect the federal government to spend about £100–120 billion, the biggest portion of which would be on debt interest.[9] The federal budget would also include the EU gross contribution.

The amount spent at the federal level would be roughly equal to the UK VAT yield or the UK national insurance yield or about two-thirds of the UK income tax yield. It is important that there are broad legal constraints on federal taxation that can only be changed by agreement of the Scottish and RUK parliaments. The principle that should be followed is that taxes can be levied by the federal government with the following constraints:

- A value added tax can be levied at a set maximum rate with a broad base.

8   Unlike in the case of the euro, this provision would be enforceable because the central bank would not be taking Scottish or RUK debt in monetary operations and therefore becoming liable for default through the back door.

9   Interestingly, this takes us very close to the position in 1870 when UK government spending was 10 per cent of national income, about half of which was debt interest. Indeed, a key reason for a federal approach is that it recognises that, when the welfare state was developed, it could have been developed independently for Scotland and the rest of the UK. Broadly, as already noted, the proposed federal government will undertake those functions that governments undertook for most of the period of the Union (from 1714 to the development of the welfare state in 1911).

- A land value tax or tax on imputed rent can be levied, the maximum rate of which is linked to the lower of the basic rates of income tax levied in Scotland and RUK (e.g. a land value tax of one-twentieth of the lowest basic rate of income tax).
- Any property tax that is levied applies equally to business and domestic property.

It is preferable not to levy a federal income tax given the link between income tax and the corporation tax system that would be administered separately in the two countries, but a federal income tax should not be ruled out on principle.

Objections to a federal solution

Gough and Tyrie (2015) object to a federal solution. They describe it as an 'attractive, tidy and apparently logical' solution but argue that it could not be implemented quickly. Further, they suggest that the size of England (or RUK as proposed here) would make the UK an unequal federal partnership for which there is no precedent. The main objection appears to be that the federal government would be a weak and marginal player in domestic affairs and that the solution would not hold.

These are not compelling objections. The whole purpose of the proposed federal arrangement is to ensure that the UK government does become a marginal player in domestic affairs. This would enable foot voting, competition and a better matching of the provision of public goods and regulation to the views and preferences of the citizens of the nations involved. There is some merit in the point regarding the issue of the size of RUK or England relative to Scotland. However, this differential exists in the case of Westminster representation currently – it is simply a matter of population and geography. With regard to issues such as defence and foreign affairs, which are currently issues for the Westminster parliament and will become the responsibility of a federal parliament, Scotland currently holds fewer than 10 per cent of all the votes. Exactly how representation should be determined in the proposed federal parliament is a practical problem beyond the scope of this paper but, no doubt, Scottish representation would be around 10 per cent of the total or perhaps higher.

The main political advantage of a federal solution is the stability that comes from government by consent combined with an alignment between taxation, representation and decision-making. The fact that there will be between two and four countries within the federal arrangement should make decision-making under unanimity relatively easy, thus aiding the stability of the arrangements further.

There have been other criticisms of federal government. For example, some studies have suggested that unitary governments can perform better than federal governments. However, this may be because in some federal systems accountability is not clear. The proposals made here involve much clearer accountability and delineation of responsibilities than exist under the current unitary system of government or under any feasible unitary system that could exist in the future given the desire to decentralise more authority to Scotland, and possibly other areas of the UK. It is also possible that federal systems originate from internal conflict (including armed conflict) within a country and that the internal conflict is the underlying source of lack of prosperity. It is therefore difficult to compare like with like when looking at the performance of federal and unitary systems.

7 FURTHER FISCAL DECENTRALISATION: SPENDING AND REGULATORY RESPONSIBILITIES

The creation of a federal UK is only part of the necessary decentralisation agenda. Within individual nations, there should be further decentralisation. It would be for the individual nations to decide how much further to decentralise policy within their own jurisdictions. However, local government funding in Wales and Northern Ireland is already a devolved matter and it will be assumed that this remains the case. In effect, therefore, what follows is a discussion of the decentralisation of government in England, though the author believes that it would be beneficial for Scotland, Wales and Northern Ireland to follow a similar track.

Principle to be followed

The principle that should be followed is that there should be the widest possible decentralisation of both spending and fiscal responsibilities to the lowest level of government that is consistent with the efficient provision of public goods. Given that local authority areas can combine to provide services, and smaller units of local government can contract with bigger units for the latter to provide services, there should be a bias *in favour* of over-decentralisation.

The principle that should be followed in essence is that of subsidiarity, which is an aspect of Catholic social teaching much misquoted and misused in relation to the EU (see Chapter 1).

As already noted, the principle argues that smaller organisations should be allowed to do what they can do, not what they are most efficient at doing – this also implies that the benefit of the doubt should be in the direction of decentralisation. The principle of subsidiarity as used in the EU is quite different.[1] This allows the EU to act in the field of regulation and other interventions if it believes it would be more effective than if action is taken by member states. In the document explaining the concept, it also states that action should only be taken at the local level if action at the local level is necessary. In general, the principle of subsidiarity as used in the EU is wide open to interpretation and the document defining it seems contradictory. However, the principle does have a very clear meaning in its original form and that should be the meaning adopted when it comes to the programme of decentralisation in the UK.

Fiscal decentralisation within England should broadly follow the proposals of Packer and Sinclair (2015). Substantial additional responsibilities would be passed to

---

1   http://eur-lex.europa.eu/legal-content/EN/TXT/?uri=uriserv:ai0017

county councils, cities with county powers and unitary authorities. However, the basic unit of local government could – indeed should – hand down responsibility further to parishes, towns or district council areas.

Consider, for example, the situation of parish councils that currently have tiny budgets. Lindfield, a large parish council area in Sussex, has a budget of £200,000, which amounts to £33 per head of population.[2] Most local authority spending for Lindfield residents is undertaken at county council level. The relevant county, West Sussex, has an area of nearly 800 square miles and a population of nearly one million. It is implausible that nearly all goods and services that cannot be provided privately by individuals and families and which need to be provided by some layer of sub-central government need to be provided on such a centralised and large scale by a county council.

The precise method by which there could be further decentralisation is not discussed here. However, there are three potential approaches that could be followed:

- The basic local authority unit could devolve further powers (with agreement) to district and parish council levels.
- The lower levels could be given statutory responsibilities and tax raising powers by central government (as happens now) but with these responsibilities being much wider than those currently held.

2   http://www.lindfieldparishcouncil.gov.uk/Core/LindfieldPC/UserFiles/Files/FGPMins08.01.15.pdf

- Lower levels of local authority could ask for powers to be granted, and this could be agreed by the Secretary of State.

Decentralisation in practice

Working from the above principles, the policy areas to be devolved to local government level should include environmental policy, aspects of welfare, education and health, policing and certain forms of regulation. There are other areas of policy that should also be considered for decentralisation, for example, road building, ownership and maintenance (see Knipping and Wellings 2012). The list discussed here should not be considered exhaustive.

There should also be a review of all statutory requirements on local authorities.[3] The only ones that would be retained would be those necessary to prevent local authorities shifting burdens onto neighbouring areas and those that involved, for reasons of efficiency, local authorities executing central government functions (for example, registrar functions).

Environmental policy

Most areas of environmental policy should be dealt with at local level, including by local authorities combining together. Problems such as flood defences, whether to manage environmental problems or prevent them, and so

---

3   In 2011 there were over 1,300 such statutory duties as discussed above.

on, are best dealt with at the local level, where local preferences about the costs and benefits in the context of different geographies and population densities can be taken into account.

Working-age welfare

Working-age welfare is a strong candidate for localisation. While it may be desirable for central government to provide a minimum income for those in greatest need, other aspects of working-age welfare should be localised. It has been proposed by Niemietz (2012), for example, that working-age benefits for those not working a full week should be attached to strong work requirements. Local authorities should manage benefits for these groups and administer training and work requirements. The situation and needs of the unemployed in, for example, Cambridge, are very different from the situation and needs of the unemployed in Doncaster or Cornwall, and these needs could be best managed locally with financial responsibility at local level.

Such an approach has been tried in Lithuania and has met with considerable success in reducing the number of people who receive welfare and the average amount paid to recipients. Local authorities have an incentive to create the right business conditions for job creation and for the promotion of prosperity more generally and also to finance or provide the right kind of programmes for those who are at the margins of the labour market. Though it is difficult to make a judgement about the reform so soon after its implementation in 2014, the performance of a pilot group of local authorities in which the programme was implemented in 2011 does indicate success. There are also very strong signs of success elsewhere in the country in the first year of the reform.[4]

Part of the Clinton reforms of welfare benefits in the US in 1996 involved giving greater financial responsibility to states. There were a large number of other changes undertaken at the same time and so it is difficult to measure the success of one particular change. However, some states, taking the opportunity to innovate within their welfare systems, were extremely successful when it came to moving welfare recipients into work. The basic problem is that the needs of those without full-time work are very diverse. In some areas, there may be structural problems causing long-term unemployment; in other areas a large proportion of the unemployed may have difficulty with language skills or have received a very poor education; others may have problems with addiction; and so on. These problems are more likely to be identified and resolved at local level with the right incentives in place for local government to devise effective welfare systems.

Education and health

In the case of education, there should be complementary reform that would promote the maximum degree of

---

4   http://en.llri.lt/wp-content/uploads/2015/07/Social-Allowances-across
     -Municipalities.pdf

autonomy for parents. However, certain residual issues such as ensuring special needs provision (though not necessarily providing it), making sure that schools that are receiving state-funded vouchers[5] fulfil the requirements of the law, and so on would be a local authority function. The general financing of education would be removed entirely from local authority budgets and be directed through parents. However, local authorities would have discretion, for example, to finance free school meals, adult education courses, special education and training courses for those not in employment, and provide support for higher education institutions. These would be entirely a matter for the local authority – as would be decisions as to whether to charge those outside the local authority area for such provision.

With regard to healthcare, again there should be complementary reforms to promote much greater individual choice, but there might be some functions that are currently undertaken nationally that should be undertaken by local government. These might include public health functions, for example.

Natural resource exploitation

Currently, all natural resources below ground are assumed to be owned by the Crown. The UK government gives licences to extract such resources and normally takes a royalty in the form of taxes. This system has several

---

5   Assuming that vouchers or some similar system would be the preferred system of giving parental autonomy over education.

disadvantages over the system that exists in the US and existed in the UK before the Petroleum Production Act 1934. Historically, in the UK – and still today in the US – natural resources were owned by landowners. Landowners then had an incentive to exploit resources to an extent that was economic, subject to meeting local planning rules that might try to prevent pollution, unsightly extraction works and so on. This is one reason for the success of the fracking industry in the US and the success of the coal industry in nineteenth- and early-twentieth-century Britain compared with the relative failure of the UK fracking industry in the last few years.

Central government ownership of resources immediately creates conflict. The government owns the royalty raised in the form of taxes from the exploitation of resources, but the local people suffer the cost. If the resources were privately owned, the owner would be able to compensate those affected directly in return for being given planning permission to extract the resources.

The localisation of extraction rights for oil and gas within local councils would achieve many of the benefits of returning rights to the owners of the property below which extraction was taking place. It would then be local residents who would both bear the cost and gain any royalties or taxes from resource extraction and thus economically rational decisions could be made, with direct compensation being provided to affected groups if necessary. It is therefore proposed that all onshore gas and oil exploitation rights should lie with local authorities, though local authorities could privatise such rights if they wished.

Lifestyle regulation

The arguments for decentralisation also apply to regulation. Although the author would prefer to reduce the extent of regulation in general, the power to regulate would clearly still exist within government. However, the government should divest itself of such powers in relation to a large number of areas. Broadly, these areas would involve the provision of non-tradable services and other controls on lifestyles. For example, the following would become the responsibility of local government:

- all aspects of alcohol licensing provisions and licensed premises opening times
- regulations in relation to smoking in private places (such as pubs and cafés) and public places (such as streets and local-government-owned parks)
- provisions related to gambling
- shop opening hours (including Sunday trading rules)

There has been a great deal of controversy about such issues in recent years. However, there is no reason why decisions about such matters should take place at national level. Taking decisions about such forms of regulation at local level would allow regulations to be better matched to local preferences and allow people to compare outcomes between regulated and deregulated areas of the country. It would allow more experimentation and copying of approaches that worked best. Localisation would also allow foot voting by those who wished to live in more liberal or more conservative local authority areas.

Policing

Currently, policing is the responsibility of directly elected police and crime commissioners covering areas that cross local authority boundaries. This is confusing for the electorate and the level of turnout in the elections for police and crime commissioners (just 15 per cent at the 2012 elections) would suggest that effective accountability in this crucial government function is low. The structure of policing is broadly determined at national level and this responsibility should be transferred to the local level. This is not only important for improving accountability, it is also important because different areas have very different policing needs.

Although responsibility should be transferred to the local level, it does not follow that there should be a police authority in every local government area. It is important that local governments can form police authorities with neighbouring areas because of the mobile nature of crime and because of the awkward geographical shape of some local authorities: Buckinghamshire, for example, is just ten miles wide at its narrowest point.

However, the principles expressed above suggest that local authorities should have clear accountability and responsibility for policing. This would not stop local authorities combining together to create regional police forces, but such decisions should be taken by local authorities themselves so that it is clear to electors who should be held responsible for performance. Indeed, Buckinghamshire has a joint fire authority with Milton Keynes, a decision that belongs in the hands of the two local authorities (a county council and unitary authority, respectively) and not the national government. A similar approach could be followed with policing.

Housing and planning

The RUK government could retain a role providing cash support for individuals who cannot afford housing. With regard to the provision of housing, local authorities would be free to build homes, though definitely not encouraged to do so. Furthermore, they would have to do so within the financial constraints proposed below.

However, local authorities should have much greater freedom when it comes to land-use planning systems. If this function were localised, which would involve the repeal of the Town and Country Planning Act 1947, there would be strong incentives for local authorities to introduce market-based planning systems through which residents would be compensated for the loss of environmental amenities when development takes place. Such an approach would give local authorities an incentive to grow the tax base, ensure an alignment of the interests of residents and developers and help ensure that development balanced efficiency and environmental costs in a rational way.

8 FURTHER FISCAL DECENTRALISATION: REVENUE RAISING

Local authority revenue-raising requirements

As has been discussed above, fiscal decentralisation must take place in respect of both taxation and spending if it is to be effective. With some possible exceptions discussed below, spending in the local authority area should be entirely met from taxes raised locally. A crucial principle is that local authorities must be able to decide both the level of taxes and which taxes to levy, within some loose limits.

This immediately leads to the question of how much money would have to be raised locally. A trivial increase in the amount that has to be raised does not necessarily lead to important questions about the appropriate tax base, but a significant increase would do so.

Currently, business rates raise around £27bn and council tax around £28bn, a total of £55bn.[1] Business rates are currently collected and set nationally, though this system is set to be liberalised a little. Around half of the business rate total is absorbed into general government revenue streams,

---

1 http://budgetresponsibility.org.uk/pubs/March2015EFO_18-03-webvl
   .pdf

which helps finance central government grants to local authorities, and the other half is retained by local authorities.

It is difficult to define relevant local authority expenditure precisely because some is financed by specific grants and user charges. However, business rates and council tax make up roughly half of all local government spending in England. At first sight, in order to maintain spending at current levels, local authorities would need to double their revenue raising to around £100bn even if they had total control of business rates. However, it has been proposed that mainstream schools' funding will be directed through parents to schools, bypassing the local authority financing system altogether. This would reduce total local authority spending by £30bn.[2] Although it has also been proposed that local authorities should become responsible for working-age welfare, this would be financed through central government (see below). Overall, it would appear that a modest total increase in local government revenue raising would be necessary, perhaps of the order 25 per cent.

Local authority revenue sources

As Packer and Sinclair (2015) suggest:

> The objective for local taxes should be that they align the incentives of sub-national government with the economic interests of the wider community.

---

2   https://www.gov.uk/government/statistics/la-and-school-expenditure
    -financial-year-2012-to-2013

This may be achieved by changing the tax base to one which is broader and also involves levies on natural resource exploitation. A narrow tax base can lead to local authorities attempting to raise taxes on one part of the electorate to finance spending that will benefit other parts of the electorate and thus lead to rent seeking. Indeed, this problem was presciently anticipated by Bastable (1895) in his great work on public finance. The use of a broad tax base should also ensure that the local authority has an incentive to provide good conditions for businesses to flourish as well as ensuring that local authorities can reap the benefits of migration rather than just the costs. For the reasons explained by Packer and Sinclair (2015), capital taxes would be very difficult to administer at local level. Arguably the same applies to income tax – see below.

Further details are beyond the scope of this Readings, but it is proposed that, in principle, local authorities should mainly raise revenue from a combination of a broad-based consumption tax, property and land taxes and some other levies. The property tax should not be progressive but should be approximately proportional to the value of the property and it should be paid directly by tenants or explicitly charged by landlords to tenants. There should also be a fixed relationship between residential and business property taxes. This would mean that any increase in spending would necessitate a rise in the taxes paid by the whole resident population at least to some extent. As discussed above, a tax specifically on tourists could help finance public goods for tourists. This could take the form of a levy on hotel occupancy.

In summary, the following tax options should be available to local authorities:

- taxes modelled on the current council tax
- land value taxes
- taxes on business property
- natural resource levies
- consumption taxes
- tourist taxes

In addition, local authorities could be allowed to vary the rate of income tax, though this would be collected by central government and redistributed to local authorities. There would be difficulties in using local income taxes because of the difficulties involved in defining residence for those with more than one dwelling (see Bastable 1895). This is a problem that causes difficulties for national authorities and would cause even more difficulties within a nation.

Realistically, district councils and other lower-level authorities such as parishes would have to finance their spending through a precept on a tax that was easy to vary according to the place of residence of the individual such as one of the property taxes.

Local authorities would also have the power to reduce taxes for groups of residents and businesses that wished to opt out of local services and provide their own services.

Redistribution

One of the justifications for the centralised system of government in the UK is the need for redistribution. Currently, the government works out the resources each local authority area should need in order to provide a given set of services and then deducts the amount that can be raised locally through a given level of taxes. The idea of the redistribution system is that each local government area should be able to provide the same level of services with the same level of taxes.

It is worthwhile comparing two local authorities in order to illustrate the level of redistribution as well as the scale of local authority support from central government more generally. Birmingham City Council spends a total of just over £3bn. About two-thirds of this is made up of central government transfers or grants of various kinds (including the uniform business rate).[3] Dorset County Council spends around £267m, of which nearly £200m (nearly three-quarters) is financed by council tax.[4] There have been various forms of redistribution within the local government finance system since 1929 (see Sandford 2014).

The degree of redistribution within the local government system has increased as the need for it has decreased.

---

3   See http://www.birmingham.gov.uk/cs/Satellite?blobcol=urldata&blobhe ader=application%2Fpdf&blobheadername1=Content-Disposition& blobkey=id&blobtable=MungoBlobs&blobwhere=1223582655783&ssbi nary=true&blobheadervalue1=attachment%3B+filename%3D8292Coun cil_Tax_Booklet_2015.pdf. Of course, even an area which is receiving government grants may simply be receiving money back that citizens have paid in general taxes (in the same way as the UK government receives grants from the EU out of the general pool of taxes that comprises the EU's resources). However, the important point is to match revenue-raising and spending responsibilities more closely.

4   https://www.dorsetforyou.com/article/418043/Dorset-County-Council -Tax-201516

Much welfare and health provision was previously provided at the local level and is now financed and provided nationally. It is also proposed above that education is removed from local government finance, with funds effectively being raised by central government and provided directly to parents. In short, if people are poor, then the general provision of income top-ups by government will provide for such needs. Furthermore, finance for health and education would be provided nationally on a basis determined by the RUK government and this could include higher levels of support, for example, for poorer parents. It is not clear that further redistribution is necessary except in very particular circumstances to a small number of local authorities.

Following this logic, there is one area of spending for which the relevant taxes should not be raised locally: working-age welfare. A local authority area with high levels of working-age welfare claimants is also likely to have a low tax base. Any minimum income to be received by individuals should be determined by national and not local government and financed from national government taxes.[5] However, the management of working-age welfare would be devolved in order to take advantage of local knowledge and local differences. To set in place the right incentive structures, it is also important to ensure that the cash grant to local authorities to top up the incomes of, and provide services to, those on working-age

---

5   The national government may wish to vary the minimum income according to the cost of living in different local areas.

welfare is fixed in advance so that any gains from successful programmes accrue to local authorities. The principles that should be followed are that the function should be devolved and should be financed nationally, but that working-age welfare should be financed in such a way that local areas benefit from managing the problem effectively.

Local government borrowing rules

Currently, most local authority borrowing is guaranteed by the UK government through the Public Works Loan Board. In return, there are considerable powers of intervention by government in the finances of local authorities. It would be preferable if central government did not guarantee debt and if there were less intervention in local government debt management.

The principle should be established that, in general, local authorities can borrow for capital projects, but that they must be entirely responsible for that debt. If a local authority could not repay debt, it would find it difficult to raise further money for capital projects, but current spending should not be affected if this is financed entirely through taxation. Local authorities could also raise funds by securitising revenues from investment projects (for example, by issuing bonds, to be serviced by road tolls).

As far as current spending is concerned, it is reasonable to expect local authorities to keep reserves to deal with cyclical fluctuations in revenue but some borrowing could be permitted (for example, up to 5 per cent of current spending in any given year with a maximum debt level of 10 per cent of spending). It may be reasonable to have backstop limits on debt for both capital and current expenditure. However, a firmly established no-bailout principle is more important than government rules about the level of debt (see Blankart 2015). In a major study, Rodden (2006) shows that successful decentralisation requires that sub-central levels of government have their own sources of general purpose tax revenue[6] and also that it is common knowledge to voters that local government is responsible for its own debts. This principle must be established strongly, both for local government and for Scotland and RUK – there should be no federal responsibility for the debts of any other governmental unit. There should also be no national responsibility (RUK, Scotland, etc.) for local government debts.

---

6   Alternatively, the central government should dominate taxation and regulate borrowing, which has, of course, been ruled out as an option.

9 CONCLUSION

The UK is a very centralised state. This is especially so for a country that is so large in terms of both population and national income. Indeed, among the G7, it is easily the most centralised country as measured by the proportion of taxation raised below central government level. Government spending is also very centralised in Britain, and, furthermore, local government is heavily constrained or directed by central government regulation.

Economic performance could be improved significantly not only through the decentralisation of revenue raising but also through more decentralisation of spending decisions and regulatory functions. Furthermore, a process of decentralisation of responsibility to the local level would help ensure that services and regulation were better matched to local preferences and circumstances. It would also create greater competition between local authorities: voters could move from one local authority to another if their own authority was ineffective. The erosion of the tax base that would result from such decisions would provide the right incentives for local government to be efficient and effective. Empirical evidence confirms the theoretical work and suggests that decentralisation would be especially beneficial in the UK context.

Current UK government proposals to devolve power to local government are piecemeal, arbitrary, do not involve proper local fiscal responsibility and may well lead to the centralisation of political power at a higher level of local government than exists currently.

Wide-ranging responsibilities should be moved from central government to local government level. These would include areas such as lifestyle regulation, welfare for those of working age, policing, housing and land-use planning and natural resource exploitation. Other policy areas such as health and education may require some limited local government oversight, but responsibility in these fields should be decentralised further to civil society and families, with the government maintaining a role in providing finance.

It is essential that incentives are properly aligned within any reform. Local government should raise taxes to finance all its functions, other than welfare for people of working age, which would be financed by a fixed central government grant. A variety of tax options would be available but it is important that, in principle, taxes are raised from a wide base to prevent citizens demanding spending financed by a narrow group of taxpayers. Also, just as responsibility for the regulation of natural resource extraction should lie with local government, local government should decide whether and how to tax natural resource revenues and it should receive any such taxes.

In addition to government being far too centralised in the UK, the current devolution settlement is unstable.

There is a bias in favour of bigger government and a high degree of representation without taxation within Westminster. This has arisen because devolution has been granted to Scotland, Wales and Northern Ireland and yet members of parliament from those nations sit in the UK parliament and can vote on issues that do not affect their constituents. Indeed, the Celtic nations are actually over-represented in the UK parliament in relation to their population when it might be expected that they would be under-represented. These problems will be exacerbated as the government's proposals for further devolution are implemented.

Various solutions to the problems within the UK's system of governance have been proposed. However, they tend to be impractical, add another layer of government, add complexity to the system or do not solve the problems inherent within the current system. Indeed, some of the proposals have two or more of these shortcomings.

The UK should become a federal country. Most responsibilities should be transferred to Scotland and either RUK or England, Wales and Northern Ireland separately. The federal government would have very few functions, including defence, border control and foreign affairs. Separate revenue streams would be raised at the federal level through federal taxes.

This approach would return the UK government to performing the kind of functions that it performed for most of the period since the Union before so much government intervention in economic life became the norm. It should be attractive to those who believe in small government, those who believe in localism and also, as a 'second-best' option to those who support independence for Scotland (or England, Wales and Northern Ireland).

In light of the experience of other federal systems, which have seen a tendency for powers to flow back to the centre over time, there would be mechanisms put in place to prevent re-centralisation. It is suggested that unanimity be required among the federal government and the Scottish and RUK governments before powers are transferred to the federal level. The federal parliament would be small and meet much less frequently than the current UK parliament. The number of federal government departments would also be very small.

Crucially, there should be an explicit compact between the federal government and the Scottish and RUK governments that the former will never bail out the latter, either explicitly, or implicitly through the central bank. Similarly, local government would never be bailed out. Together with the effective alignment of revenue-raising and spending powers, this principle must be at the heart of any devolution and decentralisation process that aims to ensure stability, accountability and prudent fiscal management at all levels of government.

The guiding principle of all these proposals would be that of subsidiarity. Defined properly, this means that power should be exercised at the lowest level possible. In general, the bias should be in favour of over-decentralisation.

REFERENCES

Ashworth, J., Galli, E. and Padovano, F. (2013) Decentralization as a constraint to Leviathan: a panel cointegration analysis. *Public Choice* 156: 491–516.

Bastable, C. F. (1895) *Public Finance.* London: Macmillan.

Bevan,G.,Karanikolos,M.,Exley,J.,Nolte,E.,Connolly,S.andMays, N. (2014) *The Four Health Systems of the United Kingdom: How Do They Compare?* London: The Health Foundation and Nuffield Trust. http://www.nuffieldtrust.org.uk/sites/files/nuffie ld/140411_four_countries_health_systems_full_report.pdf

Blankart, C. (2015) Swiss role – what the euro zone could learn from Switzerland. *Economic Affairs,* Spring. London: Institute of Economic Affairs.

Blöchliger, H. (2013) Decentralisation and economic growth. Part 1. How fiscal federalism affects long-term development, Working Papers on Fiscal Federalism 14. Paris: OECD.

Blöchliger, H. and Pinero Campos, J. M. (2011) Tax competition between sub-central governments, Economics Department Working Paper 872. Paris: OECD. http://www.oecd-ilibra ry.org/docserver/download/5k4559gx1q8r.pdf

Bolick, C. (1994) *European Federalism: Lessons from America.* Occasional Paper 93. London: Institute of Economic Affairs.

Booth, P. M. and Morrison, A. (2012) Promoting a free market by ending the single market – reforming EU financial regulation, *Economic Affairs* 32(3): 24–31.

Caplan, B. (2007) *The Myth of the Rational Voter – Why Democracies Choose Bad Policies.* Princeton University Press.

Cotarelli, C. (2009) Macro policy lessons for a sound design of fiscal decentralization. International Monetary Fund. https://www.imf.org/external/np/pp/eng/2009/072709.pdf

Cuenca, A. (2009) Estabilidad presupuestaria y endeudamiento económico en la crisis. *Cuadernos de Derecho Público* 38 (September–December): 161–75.

De la Fuente, Á. (2012) El nuevo modelo sistema de financiación de las Comunidades Autónomas de régimen común: un análisis crítico y datos homogéneos para 2009 y 2010. Documento de Trabajo 12/23, November. Madrid: BBVA Research.

Fernández-Llera, R. (2009) Estabilidad presupuestaria, transparencia y concierto económico vasco. *Ekonomiaz* 70(1): 356–87.

Gough, R. and Tyrie, A. (2015) *Voice and Veto – Answering the West Lothian Question.* Report. London: Centre for Policy Studies.

Hayek, F. A. (1990) *The Denationalisation of Money.* Hobart Paper 70. London: Institute of Economic Affairs.

Heywood, P. (2000) Spanish regionalism: a case study. Report prepared for the Constitution Unit, University College London.

Kirzner, I. (1992) *The Meaning of Market Process, Essays in the Development of Modern Austrian Economics.* London: Routledge.

Knipping, O. and Wellings, R. (2012) *Which Road Ahead – Government or Market?* Hobart Paper 171. London: Institute of Economic Affairs.

Lyons, M. (2007) Place shaping: a shared ambition for the future of local government. The Lyons Inquiry into Local Government. Report. London: The Stationery Office.

Mellows-Facer, A. (2006) Local Elections 2006. House of Commons Research Paper 06/26. London: House of Commons Library.

Niemietz, K. (2012) *Redefining the Poverty Debate – Why a War on Markets Is No Substitute for a War on Poverty.* Research Monograph 67. London: Institute of Economic Affairs.

Ofsted (2013) Report of Her Majesty's Chief Inspector of Education, Children's Services and Skills. Manchester: Ofsted. https://www.gov.uk/government/uploads/system/uploads/attachment_data/file/386795/Ofsted_Annual_Report_2012 13_Schools.pdf

Olson, M. (1965) *The Logic of Collective Action.* Cambridge, MA: Harvard University Press.

Packer, T. and Sinclair, M. (2015) *Slicing up the Public Sector – A Radical Proposal for Devolution.* Discussion Paper 59. London: Institute of Economic Affairs.

Ricketts, M. (2004) Economic analysis and inter-jurisdictional competition, *Economic Affairs* 24(1): 28–33.

Rodden, J. A. (2006) *Hamilton's Paradox: The Promise and Peril of Fiscal Federalism.* Cambridge University Press.

Rodriguez-Pose, A. and Ezcurra, R. (2011) Is fiscal decentralization harmful for economic growth? Evidence from the OECD countries. *Journal of Economic Geography* 11(4): 619–43.

Ruiz Almendral, V. (2002) Fiscal federalism in Spain: the assignment of taxation powers to the Autonomous Communities. *European Taxation* 42(11): 467–75.

Ruiz Almendral, V. (2004) The asymmetric distribution of taxation powers in the Spanish State of the Autonomies: the common system and the *foral* tax regimes. *Regional and Federal Studies* 13(4): 41–66.

Ruiz Almendral, V. (2012) Sharing taxes and sharing the deficit in Spanish fiscal federalism. *eJournal of Tax Research* 10(1): 88–125.

Ruiz Almendral, V. and Cuenca A. (2009) Estabilidad presu-puestaria en las Comunidades Autónomas: más allá de la reforma de la Constitución. *Cuadernos de Información Económica* 241, July–August: 35–44.

Sandford, M. (2014) *English Local Government Finance: Issues and Options*, Research Paper 14/43. London: House of Commons Library.

Sinclair, M. (2014) Taxpayers for fiscal decentralisation. In *A U-Turn on the Road to Serfdom* (ed. G. Norquist). Occasional Paper 150. London: Institute of Economic Affairs.

Smith, D. B. (2006) *Living with Leviathan – Public Spending, Taxes and Economic Performance*. Hobart Paper 158. London: Institute of Economic Affairs.

Somin, I. (2013) *Democracy and Political Ignorance – Why Smaller Government Is Smarter*. Stanford University Press.

Somin, I. (2014) Foot voting, federalism and political freedom. In *Federalism and Subsidiarity* (ed. J. E. Fleming and J. T. Levy), Nomos LV, Yearbook of the American Society for Political and Legal Philosophy, New York University Press.

Speer, S. (ed.) (2014) *Quebec's Government Indebtedness: Unnoticed, Uncontrolled*. Vancouver: Fraser Institute.

Thießen, U. (2003) Fiscal decentralisation and economic growth in high-income OECD countries. *Fiscal Studies* 24(3): 237–74.

Tiebout, C. M. (1956) A pure theory of local expenditures. *Journal of Political Economy* 64(5): 416–24.

Tullock, G. (1976) *The Vote Motive*. Hobart Paperback 9. London: Institute of Economic Affairs.

Vaubel, R. (2009) *European Institutions as an Interest Group – The Dynamics of Ever Closer Union*. Hobart Paper 167. London: Institute of Economic Affairs.

ABOUT THE IEA

The Institute is a research and educational charity (No. CC 235 351), limited by guarantee. Its mission is to improve understanding of the fundamental institutions of a free society by analysing and expounding the role of markets in solving economic and social problems.

The IEA achieves its mission by:

- a high-quality publishing programme
- conferences, seminars, lectures and other events
- outreach to school and college students
- brokering media introductions and appearances

The IEA, which was established in 1955 by the late Sir Antony Fisher, is an educational charity, not a political organisation. It is independent of any political party or group and does not carry on activities intended to affect support for any political party or candidate in any election or referendum, or at any other time. It is financed by sales of publications, conference fees and voluntary donations.

In addition to its main series of publications the IEA also publishes a quarterly journal, *Economic Affairs*.

The IEA is aided in its work by a distinguished international Academic Advisory Council and an eminent panel of Honorary Fellows. Together with other academics, they review prospective IEA publications, their comments being passed on anonymously to authors. All IEA papers are therefore subject to the same rigorous independent refereeing process as used by leading academic journals.

IEA publications enjoy widespread classroom use and course adoptions in schools and universities. They are also sold throughout the world and often translated/reprinted.

Since 1974 the IEA has helped to create a worldwide network of 100 similar institutions in over 70 countries. They are all independent but share the IEA's mission.

Views expressed in the IEA's publications are those of the authors, not those of the Institute (which has no corporate view), its Managing Trustees, Academic Advisory Council members or senior staff.

Members of the Institute's Academic Advisory Council, Honorary Fellows, Trustees and Staff are listed on the following page.

The Institute gratefully acknowledges financial support for its publications programme and other work from a generous benefaction by the late Professor Ronald Coase.

The Institute of Economic Affairs
2 Lord North Street, Westminster, London SW1P 3LB
Tel: 020 7799 8900
Fax: 020 7799 2137
Email: iea@iea.org.uk
Internet: iea.org.uk

Institute of
Economic Affairs

Other books recently published by the IEA include:

Sharper Axes, Lower Taxes – Big Steps to a Smaller State
Edited by Philip Booth
Hobart Paperback 38; ISBN 978-0-255-36648-9; £12.50

Self-employment, Small Firms and Enterprise
Peter Urwin
Research Monograph 66; ISBN 978-0-255-36610-6; £12.50

Crises of Governments – The Ongoing Global Financial Crisis and Recession
Robert Barro
Occasional Paper 146; ISBN 978-0-255-36657-1; £7.50

… and the Pursuit of Happiness – Wellbeing and the Role of Government
Edited by Philip Booth
Readings 64; ISBN 978-0-255-36656-4; £12.50

Public Choice – A Primer
Eamonn Butler
Occasional Paper 147; ISBN 978-0-255-36650-2; £10.00

The Profit Motive in Education – Continuing the Revolution
Edited by James B. Stanfield
Readings 65; ISBN 978-0-255-36646-5; £12.50

Which Road Ahead – Government or Market?
Oliver Knipping & Richard Wellings
Hobart Paper 171; ISBN 978-0-255-36619-9; £10.00

The Future of the Commons – Beyond Market Failure and Government Regulation
Elinor Ostrom et al.
Occasional Paper 148; ISBN 978-0-255-36653-3; £10.00

Redefining the Poverty Debate – Why a War on Markets Is No Substitute for a War on Poverty
Kristian Niemietz
Research Monograph 67; ISBN 978-0-255-36652-6; £12.50

The Euro – the Beginning, the Middle … and the End?
Edited by Philip Booth
Hobart Paperback 39; ISBN 978-0-255-36680-9; £12.50

The Shadow Economy
Friedrich Schneider & Colin C. Williams
Hobart Paper 172; ISBN 978-0-255-36674-8; £12.50

Quack Policy – Abusing Science in the Cause of Paternalism
Jamie Whyte
Hobart Paper 173; ISBN 978-0-255-36673-1; £10.00

Foundations of a Free Society
Eamonn Butler
Occasional Paper 149; ISBN 978-0-255-36687-8; £12.50

The Government Debt Iceberg
Jagadeesh Gokhale
Research Monograph 68; ISBN 978-0-255-36666-3; £10.00

A U-Turn on the Road to Serfdom
Grover Norquist
Occasional Paper 150; ISBN 978-0-255-36686-1; £10.00

New Private Monies – A Bit-Part Player?
Kevin Dowd
Hobart Paper 174; ISBN 978-0-255-36694-6; £10.00

From Crisis to Confidence – Macroeconomics after the Crash
Roger Koppl
Hobart Paper 175; ISBN 978-0-255-36693-9; £12.50

Advertising in a Free Society
Ralph Harris and Arthur Seldon
With an introduction by Christopher Snowdon
Hobart Paper 176; ISBN 978-0-255-36696-0; £12.50

Selfishness, Greed and Capitalism: Debunking Myths about the Free Market
Christopher Snowdon
Hobart Paper 177; ISBN 978-0-255-36677-9; £12.50

Waging the War of Ideas
John Blundell
Occasional Paper 131; ISBN 978-0-255-36684-7; £12.50

Brexit: Directions for Britain Outside the EU
Ralph Buckle, Tim Hewish, John C. Hulsman, Iain Mansfield and Robert Oulds
Hobart Paperback 178; ISBN 978-0-255-36681-6; £12.50

Flaws and Ceilings – Price Controls and the Damage They Cause
Edited by Christopher Coyne and Rachel Coyne
Hobart Paperback 179; ISBN 978-0-255-36701-1; £12.50

Scandinavian Unexceptionalism: Culture, Markets and the Failure of Third-Way Socialism
Nima Sanandaji
Readings in Political Economy 1; ISBN 978-0-255-36704-2; £10.00

Classical Liberalism – A Primer
Eamonn Butler
Readings in Political Economy 2; ISBN 978-0-255-36707-3; £10.00

Other IEA publications

Comprehensive information on other publications and the wider work of the IEA can be found at www.iea.org.uk. To order any publication please see below.

Personal customers

Orders from personal customers should be directed to the IEA:

Clare Rusbridge
IEA
2 Lord North Street
FREEPOST LON10168
London SW1P 3YZ
Tel: 020 7799 8907. Fax: 020 7799 2137
Email: sales@iea.org.uk

Trade customers

All orders from the book trade should be directed to the IEA's distributor:

NBN International (IEA Orders)
Orders Dept.
NBN International
10 Thornbury Road
Plymouth PL6 7PP
Tel: 01752 202301, Fax: 01752 202333
Email: orders@nbninternational.com

IEA subscriptions

The IEA also offers a subscription service to its publications. For a single annual payment (currently £42.00 in the UK), subscribers receive every monograph the IEA publishes. For more information please contact:

Clare Rusbridge
Subscriptions
IEA
2 Lord North Street
FREEPOST LON10168
London SW1P 3YZ
Tel: 020 7799 8907, Fax: 020 7799 2137
Email: crusbridge@iea.org.uk